Be the Ball

Be the Ball

A Golf Instruction Book for the Mind

Charlie Jones and Kim Doren

STARK BOOKS

**Andrews McMeel
Publishing**

Kansas City

02 03 04 QUF 10 9 8 7 6 5

Library of Congress Cataloging-in-Publication Data
Jones, Charlie, 1930–
  Be the ball : a golf instruction book for the mind / Charlie Jones
  and Kim Doren.
      p. cm.
  Includes index.
  ISBN 0-7407-1090-7
    1. Golf. 2. Golf—Psychological aspects. I. Doren, Kim. II. Title.

GV965.J566 2000
796.352—dc21   00-057336

Book design by Holly Camerlinck

To Allan
For believing in us

and

To Wally
For your *animal* spirit

"Stop thinking.
Let things happen.
Be the ball."

—*Chevy Chase as Ty Webb in*
Caddyshack

Contents

Foreword

My suggestion is this: Not to read *Be the Ball* once, and not to read *Be the Ball* twice, but read this book religiously. If you read *Be the Ball* from cover to cover, naturally, you're not going to be able to absorb the whole thing. You need to come back tomorrow and read it again. Read it every day.

I tell people that obviously, you have to execute to hit a golf ball, but it's not all physical. A lot of it is mental. You'd be surprised what would happen if you were to go home, sit in a chair on your back porch and read *Be the Ball*, and then think about what it has to say. Next, repeat it in your mind. This would be as beneficial as going out to the driving range and hitting two buckets of balls.

—Lee Trevino

chapter**one**

The Mind

"You may ask what keeps
a man going when the
chips are down?
It's a journey, you animal,
not a destination. You just
keep plugging."

—*Bill Murray as
Carl Spackler in* Caddyshack

johnny**miller**

*Winner of twenty-seven PGA Tour events,
a U.S. Open in 1973, and a British Open in 1976*

When it comes right down to it, golf is the ultimate mind game, especially when you're in Sunday's final round. Even on the first day, Thursday, you have to be prepared not only to handle the shock of initial play but also to get into the flow. Once you get three or four holes under your belt you go into whatever cruise mode you're in with your game at that time.

Then comes Sunday—it's payday. That's when the mind games start. Can I hold this thing together? What do I need to do to get my best performance?

What matters is whether or not I can keep my game going, or whether I start gagging and losing it.

I always played a lot of mind games to keep myself going. I always likened my mental state on the golf course to a tachometer on a car. The yellow zone represents the peak torque line on your tachometer and the red zone is the point at which you're ready to blow up. To get maximum performance you want to get as near that red line as possible but you don't want to go over it, because if you do, parts start flying.

That's what happens to a lot of pros. They don't know how to get just up to the red line so they can get peak performance. Most guys go over it because they're trying too hard. You almost have to downplay the shots. You need to monitor the state of your nerves and then reassure yourself by saying, "Hey, I'm playing great. This is wonderful. This is super." You try to make it a real positive experience instead of feeling like you're up against the wall. I think what matters is understanding your own limitations. The greatest asset an athlete has is knowing what he's good at and what he's not good at.

You need to figure out when to go for it and when to play the chicken shots or the anti-choke shots to get the job done. A lot of times you have to win ugly. Lee Trevino was maybe the best at this. He didn't care what he looked like, he just wanted to get the job done. He would hit some ugly little low slice, then hit short of the green, chip on, two-putt, and win. It didn't look good but it worked.

I was fortunate. I didn't really choke too often from tee to green. My choking happened with my putting. For someone else, though, if the weak link of the chain is his driver, all of a sudden he'll start duck-hooking or blocking it into the bushes. If that's the case, then he has to have a semi-anti-choke shot. Maybe he just puts the driver on the ground and hits an ugly slice. He needs to have something he can do every time, under all kinds of pressure. But typically people try to hit the perfect shot instead of one that isn't so pretty but one that can be duplicated every time, no matter how much pressure there is.

For example, when I won the AT&T in 1994, I made one of the ugliest swings I've ever made on the 18th tee. I just aimed it over at the right bunker, played it back in my stance, moved up ahead of it, and hit a controlled duck hook, knowing that my worst duck hook still couldn't go far enough left to get to the ocean.

When I saw the film, my swing was really ungainly, but the bottom line is, it got the job done. I did the same thing on the second shot and knocked it on the green, two-putted, and said, "Thank you very much." I didn't have too much pride to want to look good.

Lee Trevino always says that low balls can't go too far off-line; it's the high ones that have a lot of time to get off-line. So if I start to get a little nervous, I just move the ball back in my stance and hit it low. I know I can get it on the ground quick and get the job done. As I said, you have to know your limitations.

> **"The mind is your greatest weapon.
> It's the greatest club in your bag.
> It's also your Achilles' heel."**
>
> —*Steve Elkington, 1995 PGA champion*

lee**trevino**

Winner of six major championships

I've had a hell of a time recently with my golf swing. Your swing changes all the time, but you can remember what you did when you played well. People make the mistake of going out to the driving range and hitting buckets and buckets of balls and using set after set of golf clubs and using dozens and dozens of drivers. I don't know anyone who doesn't have at least a hundred putters in his garage. But golf is more of a mind game than most people think.

Every time I start playing poorly and I can't get the ball to do anything, I sit down and do a lot of meditating. I don't go to the driving range to try to work it out, because I end up going out there and trying to correct something that's very small. It's a movement. I may have too much weight on the right side or I'm too open or too closed, or my hands may be too far back or too far forward. What I do is I sit down and picture a time when I played halfway decent and recall what I was doing.

For instance, recently I came to realize I actually had too much weight on my right side. Now, this was all done mentally. I walked out to the driving range and I put more weight on my left side and I hit the ball better than I've hit it in a year and a half. I went out and shot the easiest 68 you've ever seen.

When I arrived at the 17th hole, I was four under par and there was water on the left. I'd been hitting the ugliest hooks all week long. Have you seen the baseball players who put guards on their shins? I've got one on my left leg because I've been duck-hooking so bad I'm hitting my left shin. The 17th is a par-3 over water and I had a 5-iron out when I said, "No. No. I don't have the right club, because I'm not trusting it." I went back to my caddie and got the 6-iron and I mentally said, "Listen, dummy, trust the swing." I hit the prettiest 6-iron, about fifteen feet behind the hole. I stuck my tongue out at the water and kept on going.

At the age of sixty, I can sit in a room and figure out what I need to do, but by the time I drive to the golf course I've forgotten what it is. So now I write little notes and stick them in my pocket. I feel horrible. Everybody thinks I've got a lot of money in my pocket but they're pieces of paper—reminders such as, "Keep your head down."

I think your mind has a lot to do with the game, even more than practicing. Sure, you've got to practice until you learn all the fundamentals, but if you've been playing golf as long as I have, it's not the practice anymore, it's the mind.

tigerwoods

*Youngest man to win
all four major championships*

You have to go out there and play with everything you have. I've always been a big believer in not having any regrets. No regrets. I give it everything I have. I can honestly say this after each and every round, and each and every shot. Be proud of yourself. If you cannot say this then you're doing something wrong.

I always figure that your mind should never go wrong. You should never ever make a mental mistake. You have plenty of time to decide what you're going to do. Now if you're Joe Montana coming down the field with a three-hundred-pound lineman chasing you, you can make a mistake. You're under a lot of pressure. Someone's trying to kill you. But no one is trying to kill you in this game. You've got all the time in the world.

Physically, you can make a mistake because the golf swing is quick and a lot of things can go wrong in that one motion. But you have all the time in the world to prepare for it. That's what I believe. But that's just me. I'm a simple man.

"You can will something to happen, with your body, with your mind. The mind is that strong. You can say, 'I want to get this close to the hole.' That's where the mind comes in. The mind has to produce positive thinking. All the great players do that."

—*Byron Nelson, winner of a record eleven consecutive tournaments on the PGA Tour in 1945*

butch**harmon**

Teacher of Tiger Woods, Greg Norman, and Davis Love III

If you look at the ability level on the PGA Tour, all the players have a lot of talent. They all can play pretty good. However, the ones who have the strongest minds are usually the ones who succeed the most.

You're born with a little bit of it, and then I think you can develop it. You have to develop a mental toughness, a will to survive. If you look at the game's two greatest players, Ben Hogan and Jack Nicklaus, they had two of the best minds in golf.

That's what sets Tiger Woods apart. Obviously he has the physical ability but he's so tough mentally, too. Tiger has always been tough as far as feeling confident he could beat you. What he's learned to do is not to be as aggressive and to play smarter.

What I've tried to get him to comprehend is how Jack Nicklaus often won a golf tournament by shooting 70 or 71 on Sunday, because he had the lead and he never beat himself. Tiger now understands this and he's become even tougher mentally. I always use Nicklaus as the example, because Nicklaus was the one who had the strongest mind in modern golf.

Tiger always had the will to survive. What he didn't have was the golf smarts. He used to always try the aggressive shot but now, especially when he gets the lead, he plays much more conservatively; he doesn't beat himself. Jack Nicklaus in his heyday never beat Jack Nicklaus. There were guys who went out and played better than Jack did on a certain day, and they would win, but Jack would never beat himself. As a young man Tiger would beat himself, but now he doesn't make those mental mistakes anymore.

Tiger has matured a lot. He's grown up. He's not a twenty-year-old kid anymore. He's learned how to handle it. And he's not only matured as a golfer, but he's also matured as a human being.

I'm in my mid-fifties and I would have taken swings at half the press, because of the crap they've put him through. But, I will tell you, we had a discussion about this at the end of the '97 season and he was very fed up with it. The press was getting to him, the responsibility of being Tiger Woods was getting to him, and we had a long talk at the end of the year.

I frankly told him, "You've got two choices. You can take all the money you have right now and retire, or you can deal with it. I recommend you start dealing with it." He has, and he's done a great job. It's not easy. I travel all over the world with him and you can't believe what he has to go through. There has never been a golfer in the history of the game who has had to deal with what this kid has to deal with on a daily basis. No one even close.

"If you keep putting yourself in position to win tournaments, you're going to win a whole bunch of them."

—Butch Harmon

"I'm not going to win every tournament I play in, but I'm going to try."

—Tiger Woods, second man in history to win three majors in the same year

wally**goodwin**

Former Stanford University golf coach

At the end of the semifinals of the National Juniors in Portland, Tiger Woods hit a shot that I doubt any pro could hit. I was there. He hit a thirty-yard shot out of one trap, over another trap, to a pin that was about ten feet on his side of the green and it was stiff. You would have had to hit that shot a thousand times to know exactly what was going to happen. Nobody could believe it. But it happened right in front of me.

The only hole in Tiger's armor when he came to Stanford was from 120 yards in. When he returned from the Masters one year, we were talking about his experience and he said, "Aw, coach, I hit the ball over every green." I said, "Every green?" "Yeah, every green." I said, "Well, that's not very smart." It was interesting that when Tiger came to college that was the only problem he had.

Thank goodness Butch Harmon has been working with him. At the top of Tiger's backswing there's now a little flex in his wrist and not this hard piece of steel coming into the golf ball descending, which seemed to turn his wedge into an 8-iron.

Tiger was one of the strongest athletes here at Stanford, maybe the strongest pound for pound. He worked out every day in the weight room. He could hit all the shots. I don't have a guy on my team now who can hit all the shots. I don't have a guy on my team right now who can hit half the shots. But Tiger could hit them all.

When crunch time came, Tiger Woods knew several things. He knew, "I've come from behind a million times before. I can do it again. I'm in better shape than anybody playing. I've got an edge there. I know I can hit all the shots, because I always have, so let's get going."

It was physical before mental, but the mental aspect of playing golf, of actually swinging the golf club, is visionary. In Tiger's mind, the mental aspect of playing golf competitively was that he had the edge because he knew all of those things. In his case, he had done it so many times that anything was within the realm of possibility as long as there were holes left to play.

Tiger Woods was interesting in that he did it all with films and videos. His dad trained him with videos and when he was at Stanford he was an immense user of the videotapes he had collected over the years. His preparation for a tournament primarily involved looking at film. He would work with his wedge and his driver, but mostly he'd go back to his room and look at films.

"Tiger doesn't have much in terms of all-around athletic ability. He is a specifically trained golf athlete, the best who has ever lived."

—*Wally Goodwin*

"My analogy has been that if we were all Olympic swimmers, Tiger would be about five seconds faster than everyone in the pool."

—*Steve Elkington, two-time*
PLAYERS champion, 1991 and 1997

"Tiger is always thinking of holing out the ball.
He's not thinking, 'I'm going to get on the green,
or get close.' He's thinking of making the shot.
He thinks about it more than any other golfer.
He looks at things a little differently than
the normal player."

—Curtis Strange, back-to-back U.S. Open champion,
1988 and 1989

"There's only one way I'm going to get better.
That's to go head to head with Tiger Woods."

—Phil Mickelson, winner of the 1991
Northern Telecom Open as an amateur

annika**sorenstam**

Three-time LPGA Player of the Year, 1995, 1997, and 1998

Golf is 99 percent in your head. It's very much a mental game. It's a game where, first of all, you hit a drive and then you walk. You have a lot of thoughts in your mind. You can think of the result, such as where the ball ended up, or you can think about how you are going to hit the next shot. There is a lot of time to think between each shot before you execute it; that gives your mind time to wander.

We golf professionals think about a lot of things. A lot of amateurs get a little more stressed out in certain situations, especially a difficult shot. Fear jumps into their minds more than it does at the professional level because we put in so much more practice time.

If there's water we don't think about it. We know there's water over there, but when I make up my mind where to aim or what club to hit, I don't think about what's over there. It's just a matter of executing the shot. A lot of amateurs think about the water in the middle of their swing.

"Every single golfer struggles with the same mental challenge, and that is trying to stay mentally organized and trying not to think negative thoughts, because you have all that time to do so."

—*Glen Daugherty, head golf pro at Rancho Santa Fe Farms, California*

greg**norman**

*Winner of seventy-four tournaments
worldwide, including two British Opens*

When your golf is good, your mind is great. When your golf is bad, your mind is terrible. Right across the board. Your mind is a product of the day's results. If you're feeling good about your day, about your game, about your attitude, and about your approach to the game, it's amazing how much easier the game of golf is. The top players in the world make the game look so easy because their minds are totally relaxed. They're playing the game of golf with an unfiltered approach. They keep it very simple with such a philosophy, and that's why they just see the target, see the shot, and execute. Nothing else comes into their minds.

Truly it's that simple, because you know you've done all the right things, and you have the physical aspects of the game right. Your swing is right; therefore, your confidence is in your golf shot. You've hit all the shots you need to on the practice tee. You've seen them, you've felt them; you know you can hit the ball within a foot of where you want to hit it from 180 yards. All those things dial up the confidence mode, and once you get on the golf course you just let it go.

I think you can program your mind, but it's not as simple as merely flicking on a light switch and there it is. What happens when you are struggling with your game is you are trying to put a lot of different keys into the lock of a door in order to unlock it, but there's only one key that will work. You have to find the right key; you have to search for it. You have to look for what's going to unlock your mind and free it up.

Everybody has a different way to go about this process. It basically requires self-discipline, knowing what you've taught yourself in a practical sense over years of experience. I'm a believer in being a self-taught individual; you get out of it what you put into it and if you are tough enough in your mind, you can work through anything. I have a repertoire of sayings and mannerisms that can stimulate me. But when I run out of those, that's when I know I need to walk away from the game, take a rest, and just forget about it for a while.

> **"Once you're on the Tour, the mental part of the game is 85–90 percent."**
>
> *—David Duval, winner of the Byron Nelson Award and Vardon Trophy in 1998*

stan**thirsk**

Head pro at Kansas City Country Club for thirty-two years

Tension starts in the mind and it will destroy the feel of your swing and your confidence. The mind is where you control all your emotions. When you master your swing, it's like what Ben Hogan said: "After the 10 percent mechanics, golf is 90 percent mental and we can't control ourselves that well." That little ball is sitting there, looking up, and sticking its tongue out at you saying, "I bet you're going to mess up." And a lot of times we do.

Tension destroys the feel in your swing. It starts in your hands, in your fingers. So many people have the club up in their palms. They don't have it in their fingers, so they have to squeeze to hang on to it. They're never going to have feel.

When you write a check, you hold the pen with your fingers. When you get your car keys, you put them in the ignition with your fingers. When you unzip your bag and you take out your glove and the tee and a ball, you do it with your fingers. You don't do it with your palms.

Feel begins in the fingers. You can keep your fingers pretty snug around the handle of the club without tightening up your wrists, your forearms, or your elbows. If you can keep that tension out, you have a good chance to feel the weight in the club head and to swing it with your hands and arms.

"I don't really like too much thinking. I like to have it clear and just go ahead and hit it. Sometimes I think that if you think too much, you're thinking too many things, you're not thinking about hitting the shot."

—*Sergio Garcia, member of the 1999 European Ryder Cup team*

ken**blanchard**

Coauthor of The One Minute Manager
and founder of the Golf University

The big thing about the mind is that it's like a computer. It doesn't know the difference between the truth and what you tell it. When you put information into a computer, it doesn't say, "Where did you get this information?" It does whatever it can with the information you give it. The mind is the same way.

People come to my golf school and they'll say, "I'm awful in the sand." We'll say, "We bet you're awful in the sand." They'll say, "How do you know that?" We answer, "You just said it." You're never going to be better than you think you are. So one of the things we have them do is stand in a sand trap and say, "I'm fabulous in the sand. I'm the greatest sand-trap player in California."

Great golfers won't say, "Don't hit it in the water," because the mind doesn't know the word "don't." All the mind remembers is what you're focusing on. If you say, "Don't hit it in the water," the mind hears, "Hit it in the water." You have to tell your mind where you want the ball to go, not what you want to avoid.

Programming your mind is so important. There are three time orientations: future, present, and past. What you do behind the ball is plan the future. You say, "Okay, I want to hit it to the right of that trap," or "I'm going to hit it over there," or "I'm going to put this kind of swing on it." You're doing all your future thinking. When you approach the ball, you go into present time. That's when you get into your inner child and just be. You're into the present. You've already done the planning; your mind is loaded. You don't want to sabotage it by saying, "Keep your elbow in." You've already said that. You say that behind the ball. When you're over the ball you just want to be doing it. Then after you hit it, you move to past time and you analyze your shot.

Tim Gallwey, who wrote *The Inner Game of Golf*, says that performance is a function of ability minus interference. Interference is all those little messages you send to your mind. It's like concentrating on breathing when you're doing meditation. What you're trying to do is take your mind out of it.

I'll never forget when Jack Nicklaus won the Masters in '86. On the 16th hole he hit a fabulous shot that hit the hill and trickled down about three feet from the pin, and the place went absolutely berserk and he started to cry. He told us later, "All of a sudden I realized, 'Jack, get back in the game! You've got more holes to play! The thing's not over yet!' " The great ones are constantly dealing with their minds as much as they are with their swings.

What happens with some people is they miss a putt on the second hole because of a spike mark, and seven holes later, they're still saying, "Geez! Those damn spike marks!" One of the things that's really important is making sure that when you're behind the ball, you're planning the future, and when you're over the ball, you're in the present. After you hit it, you analyze the past and then you return to the present until it's time to do it again.

> "Golf is really a simple game. We make it complex and confusing by our approach to it."
>
> —*Greg Norman, two-time British Open champion, 1986 and 1993*

> "Get out there and do your best and don't think!"
>
> —*U.S. Solheim Cup captain Judy Rankin's advice to the 1998 U.S. team*

jack**nicklaus**

Winner of twenty major golf championships

At Augusta in 1992, I had a quadruple bogey at 12, and I had to get my act back together in a hurry. I walked off the green and mumbled, "Oh, my gosh, look what you've just done to yourself."

As I walked to the next tee I told myself, "Remember, you may have been right at the top of the leader board, but you're only six shots back. You have all these birdie holes. Go play golf. Start with your tee shot right here."

I made a great tee shot at 13, made birdie, and went on. After my second shot at 14, Jackie, my caddie, said, "Dad, that's the best golf shot I've ever seen." The pin was in the back left, which is the toughest place to get anywhere near it, and I had hit a 4-iron. It never left the flag, it just split it, and ended up two feet behind the hole. I then birdied 15 and holed a long putt at 16. That was something I had to do if I wanted to get back in the golf tournament.

You have to concentrate and work on every shot. You need to have a full, clear mind and know your parameters, your fronts, your backs, and your sides. Make up your mind about what you're trying to do and do it. If you can do that, generally everything else just disappears. You don't hear anything else.

glen**daugherty**

Head golf pro at Rancho Santa Fe Farms, California

Remember that famous putt Nicklaus holed to win the Masters over Johnny Miller and Tom Weiskopf in 1975? I always think of the par-3 16th hole. He made a putt that broke thirty feet. It was about a forty-five-footer and it broke thirty feet around the corner, over the hill, and it went in. You cannot physically calculate how to make that putt, especially under pressure. I mean, you can't make it under any circumstance. On a conscious level, you cannot make that putt. It's unmakeable. You can hit one hundred of them and none will go in.

But Nicklaus knew what he had to do to win the Masters and he knew first place was his. He was standing there and his subconscious went to work and he imagined that ball going in the hole, and then his imagination took over. It took his putter back and made the ball go in the hole. That putt is impossible to make. But he made it and won the tournament.

"When I come down the stretch, for some reason I have been able to keep myself together. My attention span gets more acute; my focus is better. I'm able to do what I'm supposed to do."

—*Jack Nicklaus,* Sports Illustrated'*s Best Individual Male Athlete of the Twentieth Century*

"If somebody plays better than I do, it never bothers me. What bothers me is when I don't prepare, when I don't get my mind on what I'm doing and I let everything else happen that keeps me from being on a positive road to where I want to go."

—*Jack Nicklaus, AP's Golfer of the Century*

"I truly believe that people like Jack Nicklaus have the ability to wear blinders when they play golf. I think these people definitely are able to play within this capsule they live in. They are not distractable people."

—*Pete Coe, head pro at La Jolla Country Club, California*

chapter**two**

The
Inner Game

"Golf's not that tough.
You've got to concentrate
about an hour and
fifteen minutes a round.
About a minute for
each shot."

*—Lee Trevino, whose first professional win
was the 1968 U.S. Open*

I was taught by Ben Hogan and Byron Nelson. They didn't know it, but they both told me the same thing. They said, "When you're practicing and you hit a good shot, don't reach over and get another ball. Watch what it does in its entirety and put that in your mind. Put that in your computer. Then when you get to a hole and have that shot, visualize it and make your muscles do it."

There were times when I felt so good over the ball, I didn't want to take it back. I knew I was going to hit it big. Even today, as seldom as I play, I'll get over the ball and say, "Pay attention to this one. This one really feels good." I don't remember when I've missed one. My mind says, "Let it go. You can do it."

The main thing is the mind. Once you have the talent, then you have to do two things: one, have the confidence to know you're going to win, and two, install that in your opponents so they know you have confidence and they know you're going to win. That's what Tiger Woods has right now.

It's like a gunfighter. Ben Hogan was the one who taught it to me. When you walk on the first tee and say, "Good morning," and shake their hands, don't look at their hands. Look them straight in the eye, and they'd better know they have their hands full, because their ass is yours.

> **"Golf is not that hard a game. We make it a lot harder than it is. Our mind gets in the way."**
>
> —*Simon Bevan, head pro at Glen Abbey Golf Club, Oakland, Ontario*

nancy**lopez**

Member of the LPGA Hall of Fame

I can't say I always expected I was going to win, but I felt I had the power to win. I really believe that. I was definitely born with the ability to go out and concentrate and focus on what I was doing. Nothing could change it because my mind was set on what I was going to do.

When I was competing and the pressure was on, I played my best golf. I was totally focused on what was happening during that time. I expected to win. I almost felt I could control it to a certain point. That was a very powerful feeling.

Being with my daughters and taking care of my family now definitely takes precedence over winning a golf tournament. I want to win, but the time I spend on my golf game compared to the time I spend with my family has really changed.

I know in my heart that if I didn't have a family and I was competing, week in and week out I would still have that fire, but I have chosen not to be so competitive because it would really affect my home life. I would be gone all year long. I would play twenty-five to twenty-eight tournaments a year instead of fourteen to sixteen. And that's okay. I could stay very competitive if I chose to do that, but I don't.

jack**lemmon**

Movie actor and passionate golfer

In a peculiar way, golf is akin to acting in a sense that you're up there and although there are other actors who are helping you by giving a good performance, by acting with you rather than at you, you are nevertheless on your own. You're giving the performance. There's no caddie saying, "Read this putt this way," or "Do this piece of business." It's up to you. It's the same in golf. There is no way you can control anything beyond what you do.

Peter Jacobsen introduced me to a golf psychologist at the AT&T a few years ago and asked him to speak to me for a few minutes. We went outside the lunch tent and started talking. He asked, "What's it like when you've got the tiger by the tail in your profession and you're really giving a great performance?" He tried to make an analogy for me. The funny thing is, it didn't work. I tried doing everything he said, and none of it worked. It should have but it didn't. I don't know why. It was like a director giving me good direction, but I couldn't take it.

One of the reasons I continue to play golf is because of what I once did that convinced me I had the potential to be a fantastic golfer. Peter Jacobsen and I were playing Brentwood Country Club, which fronts on a four-lane highway. There are two lanes coming one way and two lanes going the other way, with a divider in between, and there's always a lot of traffic. The 8th hole is a long par-5 that runs parallel to the highway. There's a huge, high fence there so if you slice, your ball won't go out onto the highway.

Well, I took my big swing and sliced it right over the top of the fence and it was gone, out in the street. So I teed it up and hit it again, and this one also went over the fence, more or less in the same spot. When I hit my third ball I aimed so far left I was practically a pretzel, and this one ended up in the fairway, thank God.

I finished the hole and then we played the short par-4 9th toward the clubhouse. I looked up after I hit my second shot and I saw the manager of the club standing by the edge of the green with a couple and two children. When I got to the green the manager said, "Oh, Mr. Lemmon, could you come here a second?"

I walked over and he said, "This is Mr. and Mrs. Such-and-Such and their children. Did you happen to hit out of bounds on the 8th?" I turned to the guy who was standing there with his wife and I said, "My God, don't tell me I hit your car." And, without missing a beat, he held up two fingers and said, "Twice!"

I figure any guy who could hit the same moving car twice, when you couldn't even see it, is a born golfer. And I've been playing my ass off ever since.

judy**rankin**

Winner of twenty-six LPGA tournaments,
recipient of the 1999 Patty Berg Award

Golf is less mind control and more emotional control. It's mind control in regard to where you *don't* let your mind go. But how golf really differs from other sports is how it affects your emotions. It's a very slow game and, unlike in most sports, you are both the action and the reaction. There's a lot of time for your mind to wear on you, a lot of time for your mind to wander, and a lot of time for doubts to creep in.

I think every great athlete has a great mind for her sport, but golf requires a little different skill. It is really important to concentrate solely on what you're doing at the present moment and not to think about winning or losing. There's a tendency to get excited about the prospect of winning or playing well. The best players are able to use that excitement to play better, whereas with other players, their excitement causes them to make poor judgments.

Most golfers have experienced true nerves, where they feel shaky. They have learned to either play around them or to overcome them. Jack Nicklaus and Nancy Lopez have both said they never, ever remember feeling nervous playing golf. They've never experienced nerves when in competition. Believe me, they are the exceptions.

"In golf, you have to learn how bad is your bad day. If you're going to be a good player, your bad day can't be very bad. You have to learn how to control those days that aren't so good."

—Judy Rankin

"This game is experimental between the ears."

—Peter Kostis, CBS golf commentator

"The average person doesn't function very well playing golf. You either have to be in the state of oneness or be able to create a state of oneness. You have to have the ability to eliminate all of the distractions and only think of one thing at a time."

—Phil Rodgers, former PGA and Senior PGA Tour player

roger**maltbie**

PGA player and golf commentator for NBC

When a golfer gets under pressure, time starts going fast. I know that seems strange for anyone who watches this game. It plods along slowly but then it starts going very quickly. It's amazing. You hit your tee shot and the next thing you know you're standing at your ball, wondering what happened.

The really great player can slow everything down and keep everything in perspective. By slowing things down, I don't mean play slowly. He can slow his thought process down and continue to think as clearly as he did before he was under stress.

The players who are less affected by adrenaline can keep things on an even keel internally. This helps not only with keeping their swing together but also for proper timing for the parts of the game that require fine motor skills: pitching, chipping, and putting.

More often than not on the PGA Tour, the players who win the events are putting well. Better than well. That's a given. But you'll see lots of players who hole putts for three and a half days and then it leaves them on Sunday afternoon. All of a sudden the putts don't go in. That's really what's more affected than anything.

When you get right down to it, golf is a game. The player who went out Thursday morning played a game, and he played a game on Friday, and he played a game on Saturday. But it's not a game on Sunday. It's real. That's what separates players in major championships. It's not a game anymore. It's bigger than that. It's important. I've always been convinced that golf isn't all that hard until you try. Once you try, it's the hardest game you'll ever play.

The same thing happens to the average player who's shooting his best score. Trust me. The feelings that the professional golfer has in the stressful situation of trying to win an event that's important to him are the very same emotions that the average 18-handicapped golfer is feeling when he's playing his best round ever. It's the same thing.

I remember when I first went on the Tour and had success and was 1975 Rookie of the Year. They told me, "Geez, it has to be so hard to win on the Tour." I said, "I don't look at it that way." It's no harder to win on the Tour than it was to win a junior golf tournament because when I was a junior, that was the most important thing to me. Winning the Salinas Junior Masters was a big deal for me! Well, winning a PGA Tour event was a big deal! They're the same. They really are.

I have to give Bob Rotella a great deal of credit for getting me back to who I am as a golfer. Everything was going great and then my teacher died, the only guy who ever taught me anything about golf. My game went into a slump, and I didn't know how to fix it. People would say, "Well, go to another teacher." But I saw all the best teachers in the game and I was getting nowhere.

So I said, "I'll try harder." I tried harder and harder and harder, and each and every day it was like I was lacing up my shoes, going to war. I was no longer myself. Tension had crept into me at horrible levels and I couldn't let go and play the game.

Bob Rotella really helped me with that. It was so logical. I remember the first time I talked to him, he asked, "What's the difference between you now and you then?" I said, "Well, I was a kid and my work ethic wasn't that good. I'm a lot more responsible now. I got married and I'm going to start a family. I'm working my heart out. I'm a lot better guy now." He just looked at me and said, "What makes you think you were wrong the other way?" I said, "Huh?" He said, "It worked, didn't it?"

My attitude back then was, if I don't play good today, so what? I'll play good tomorrow. If I don't play good tomorrow, so what? I'll play good the next day, or the next week. But all of a sudden, each and every day and each and every shot had become so important to me that it was just stifling and I couldn't get anywhere.

Bob helped me a great deal in my mission. It took me almost a year to understand it. He said, "All I want you to do is go out and have fun on the golf course. I don't care what you shoot. Your passing grade or failing grade will be if you enjoy the challenge of each and every shot and your experience of being on the golf course." Then he added, "Not most of the shots. I mean all of the shots."

I'd play three holes and I'd bogey the 4th and then I'd stroke a birdie putt on the 5th that did a 360 and lipped out. I'd start to get a little tense. I'd go to the next hole and hit one that landed eight feet from the cup, and it would suck back off the green, down the hill and I'd say with clenched teeth, "Oh, I'm having fun now!" You'd be surprised how hard this was to do for four and a half hours.

I finally got back to where I could do that, and then the game became much simpler again, much, much simpler. Tell that to Ben Hogan and he'd probably shoot you. He wouldn't understand. He'd say, "What do you mean fun? There's nothing fun about this. I put my golf ball here, I want it to go there, and that's all that matters."

My advice to the average golfer is that it's best to go have fun.

"It's not so much what you accomplish in life that really matters, but what you overcome that proves who you are, what you are, and whether you are a champion."

—*Johnny Miller, NBC golf analyst*

"A real champion is somebody who can act like a gentleman and perform like a gentleman when things are not going well."

—*Peter Jacobsen, 1990 Bob Hope Chrysler Classic champion*

deborah**graham**

Sports psychologist

We teach a three-step routine, and if you follow it for every single shot, your ability to use natural and trained skills increases significantly. The first step we teach is commitment, and players are amazed at how much better their scores get when they simply get fully committed to the shot. We ask them to commit to three things: the club, the target, and the type of shot.

Once they're fully committed we try to move them from left brain to right brain. The first part is left brain because golf is a sport where the ball is just sitting there, you're not reacting to the ball. Since the ball is stationary, you have to put yourself in the frame of mind to react. The only way to react is to get to the right brain. To do this requires the second step, visualization, which is something that stimulates the right brain.

The third step is to feel the shot. When players are playing their best, when they take a practice swing or a partial swing, they're feeling the shot they want to hit. When they aren't playing well, they're thinking of the mechanics, which is left brain, and that means they cannot react to the ball. They are now manufacturing the shot instead of creating the shot. Therefore, natural and trained skills aren't used.

We teach them this basic routine and then once they learn it, that's the foundation. Now when they're not doing well, we know more specifically what to do. We know if tension is getting in the way. We know if indecision is getting in the way, and we know if mechanics are getting in the way, all by using the three-step routine.

The best players in the world take mental breaks between shots. They do not think about the round. Their whole goal is to play one shot at a time and then leave it. That's also why the best players don't reveal how they're playing by the way they walk and the way they talk, because they let it go. Their goal is to take a break between shots, get their mind off of it so they have enough energy when they get to the next shot. If you ever finish a round exhausted, it's because you never took breaks between shots.

Do you remember the movie *Apollo 13*, with the guys floating around in their spacecraft trying to collect the millions of pieces of equipment floating around them? They get their arms full and about this time, a few slip out from under their arms and go out the back side. That's the way it is with golf. You can't get all the mechanics in place and keep them there. When one gets strong, another gets weak, so it's a real test mentally. When people who are dominant, competitive, and controlling try to control this game, it makes them crazy. You can't. You just can't control it.

"To play golf well you have to manage your focus and your concentration for four hours plus. This can be very difficult."

—*Deborah Graham*

"From a mind standpoint, there's the zone. I'm a 30 handicap and I shot an 82 one day. I felt that every ball I hit was perfect, and every putt would go in, and it did. It is a mind game, and the zone is the mind zone."

—*David Wolper, award-winning movie and television producer*

kevin**sorbo**

Television star of Hercules:
The Legendary Journeys *and avid golfer*

You'll notice how any given professional can win any given tournament on the PGA Tour on any given Sunday. That's what makes it so exciting to watch. The mind is what separates them. It's like, "Who's committed? Who's concentrating? Who's competitive? Whose attitude is the strongest that particular week?"

Golf is like art. Great art has an intrinsic lack of control. There's something about not controlling your mind, not trying to make something happen. I know that as a baseball pitcher, if I would just throw the ball, it would get across the plate. If I tried to steer it, forget it. It would hit the batter or go over his head. My acting coach used to tell me that great acting has an unpredictable quality to it and it happens when you're reacting to what's happening around you in a positive way.

The mindset is obviously very, very important for anything, whether it's golf or baseball or acting. You're going to have more success when your mind is the most clear and concise in what you are trying to do. However, you have to remember there's an unpredictable quality to anything that's great.

What makes golf so challenging is that no matter how good you are, you are never going to be perfect at it. It's impossible. It's a very addicting game. There's no question about it. I absolutely love it. I've been overdosing on it because when my *Hercules* series ended I finally had time off to play as often as I wanted to.

> **"The challenge of golf is to get the ball in the hole with the fewest strokes, not to look elegant on the driving range."**
>
> *—Pia Nilsson, head coach of the Swedish national golf team*

There's not that much difference between the players who hit it crooked and the ones who hit it straight. The statistics show that the difference between the player who is ranked first in putting and the one ranked fiftieth or the one who is most accurate from the tee versus the fiftieth is infinitesimal. The stroke average of a player who finishes 150th on the money list is within a fraction of the player who finishes in the top thirty.

The difference is that the top players know what they have to do and when they have to do it. They believe they can do it, and the others wonder if they can. The top guys expect to win.

For example, when Phil Mickelson made two double bogeys on dumb plays on Sunday at the Buick Invitational at Torrey Pines, he said afterward he knew they were dumb. But he also said, "I wasn't worried when I got to 13 and was tied with Tiger Woods, because I knew I had two par 5s left and he had only one."

He knew he could make a couple of birdies, and he knew he had two opportunities to make birdie and Tiger only had one. That kind of thinking is very different from the thinking of a lot of players. They would see a 5-, 6-, 7-shot lead evaporate in a matter of holes and then they would only be looking at the wrong things. Yes, golf is a mind game.

ron**riemer**

Director of golf equipment advertising for Golf Magazine

I believe you can get yourself into a state of mind that is calm and peaceful and relaxing, which will allow you to maximize whatever idiosyncrasies you have in your swing. For example, I'm a double-reverse Jim Furyk. He takes his club outside and then drops it in the slot. I yank it in, move it out, then I drop it into the slot. It's a compensation for a bad back. I'm the classic example of a single-digit-handicap golfer over the age of sixty. I've been a five or six for twenty-some years, and I have done it mentally.

I'm a believer in the alpha state of mind, where you get to a higher level of concentration and relaxation. I can feel it when it happens. I know that my opponents are noticing. It's a reputation I have at my club. They don't want to play me in match play, because they worry about how I'm going to make par from some godforsaken place I've hit it off the tee. From a match play standpoint, they know I have a mental edge on them.

It's a result of switching my major from business to psychology in college, being intrigued by the power of the mind, and being lucky enough to have personal acquaintances with both Chuck Hogan and Dr. Deborah Graham, who have worked with Tour players. I do all kinds of things mentally to prepare for a competitive round of golf.

First of all, the night before a round I read a couple of chapters in Arnold Palmer's book, *My Game and Yours*, which talks about the power of the mind. Then I go to bed early and get a lot of sleep. I'll get up earlier than usual so I can move a little bit slower. I'll begin to build tempo and pace and calmness in my whole being. I'll drive to the golf course a little bit slower than I normally would.

Sometimes I'll drive with my fingertips, just to prove to myself that I can control a two-thousand-pound vehicle going forty miles per hour with my fingertips, so I sure as hell don't need to grip my putter too tight on a crucial putt. Before I even get to the golf course I'm beginning to put on my game face and to work on the competitive edge. The neat thing is, my opponents know there's something going on that they can't do and I can.

In the late seventies, Chuck Hogan was working with Danny Ainge, who at the time was with the Portland Trailblazers. He was working with Danny on time sequencing, where you can mentally slow down time. Danny, although never a great scorer, was a wonderful defensive player, whose particular forte was stealing the ball off hot little point guards when they were coming down the court. Danny was working on slowing down the sequence of time so that to him, but not to anybody else, the ball was in slow motion and he could just reach in, take it, and very easily dribble away with it. It is something you can train yourself to do.

Another person to do this was Ted Williams. What made him such a great hitter? He said he could see the seams of the ball on the spin. Totally untrained, Ted Williams was doing time sequencing. He was mentally slowing down the ball and he was able to do it all by himself. Nobody back in the forties and fifties was into sports psychology, but he was able to do it. I guarantee you Ted Williams did not make that up. He truly could see the seams while the ball was spinning at ninety miles an hour. If he could do that, then he was slowing that baseball down.

Every one of us has the ability to get to the alpha state. On a graph it is portrayed as low, slow waves. It's when the alarm goes off in the morning and you hit the snooze button. You're half awake and half sleeping. Doctors and scientists have shown that in this state, your mind is the most receptive to suggestion. You can begin to program a good golf swing.

"Thinking too much about how you are doing
when you are doing is disastrous."

—Harvey Penick,
the pros' teaching pro

"Golf is largely the mindset. There are
so many people who hit the ball well but don't
get a good result because they can't think
straight. You have to realize what's what
and what's not what."

—Paul Runyon, two-time PGA champion, 1934 and 1938

chapter**three**

Thinking
It Over

"In golf, the mind
is a terrible thing."

*—Butch Harmon, personal
instructor to His Royal Majesty
King Hassan II of Morocco
and to Tiger Woods*

arnold**palmer**

*Winner of eight major championships
and ninety-two victories worldwide*

I n golf, your mind is not only responsible for momentary thinking or a momentary reaction to what you do and how it affects you, but it's also responsible for your overall training. Your mind determines how you approach the game from practice to how you develop a mindset for facing conditions that demand certain things from your body. It also controls your reaction to those demands. What happens in your mind depends on how well you train yourself, what your swing thoughts are, and how you handle tough situations.

The psychology of how you handle the back nine on Sunday when you're in contention doesn't just start Sunday afternoon. It begins before the tournament with your pretournament activity and your thoughts about how you're going to handle yourself in the tournament from the first day on. The thought that you can turn a 75 into a 69 is all part of getting yourself ready.

I can remember a lot of times when I was not playing well and I had to struggle with a bad round. You win the golf tournament by turning that bad round into a fair or modest round. A one- or two-under-par round instead of a two- or three-over-par round. The mind is responsible for all that and more.

At the 1960 U.S. Open at Cherry Hills, I knew before the tournament started that I was playing very well and my game was together. But for whatever reason, the first three rounds were worse than I expected. Interestingly, those rounds could have been even higher. However, I felt somewhere in my overall makeup I could recover from those mediocre rounds.

I was pretty frustrated when I finished the third round, and I was looking for some council, I suppose, or encouragement. I had ordered a sandwich and was just about to start eating it when I commented to Pittsburgh golf writer Bob Drum, "I think I can do something this afternoon. What do you think? If I shoot 65, will that help?" He answered, "Nothing would help you." That really pissed me off. I didn't even eat my sandwich, I went right out and hit balls on the range and when they called me to the tee I was more determined than ever. I drove the 346-yard par-4 1st green and birdied six of the first seven holes. I came from seven shots back that day to win the U.S. Open.

> **"Arnold Palmer has the best golf grip ever.
> They should take his hands and bronze them.
> His grip is even better than Harry Vardon's,
> and he invented it."**
>
> *—Lee Trevino, winner of a record five Vardon trophies*

robert**wagner**

Award-winning actor, star of Hart to Hart *and* To Catch a Thief

I oftentimes walk off the golf course thinking about the shots I missed instead of the shots I made. That's a very negative thought because you're never satisfied, and it takes you outside the moment. What's very, very important in golf is to live in the moment. There's the shot. You'll never have another shot like it again. You'll never be in the same proximity, you'll never have the same stance. Since every shot is different, the idea is to stay in that moment and not carry the last shot with you, and not project what's going to happen with the shot, but just stay within yourself.

The power of the subconscious mind is tremendous. You can take everything else out of your mind and just think about that moment, that shot. You'll get an idea of where you want the ball to go without thinking about the results, and not projecting what you want out of it. Don't say, "Oh, I've got to hit the green, I've got to do this, I've got to do that," and put all that pressure on yourself. Just set up and swing.

If you can do that with most everything in life, you'll be happy and satisfied. Keep positive, that's the philosophy I try to have, because I don't want to walk around with despair in my life, and I don't want to walk around with disappointment in my golf game. That's the way it works with me and that's the way it works with actors. You try to focus and stay in the moment. You're trying to make it be the first time and to watch your character just do it.

The most focused golfer right now is Tiger Woods. He's amazing. The thing that makes him so incredibly astounding is his focus. It's unbelievable. Focus is everything to the best athletes, the best actors, and the best musicians.

I've worked with some very fine actors, including Spencer Tracy, Laurence Olivier, and Paul Newman. When I first worked with Spencer Tracy I had to separate myself from thinking, I'm working with Spencer Tracy! I grew up sitting in a theater watching him, so I had to get it out of my head, because that's intrusion. The whole idea in acting is to get out of the way of yourself. Then you can let it go. That's what Tiger Woods does. He gets out of his own way and lets his ability take over.

> **"On the golf course I've never said, 'I'm an actor and I'm now going to play the part of a professional golfer.' But I'm willing to try anything."**
>
> —*Robert Wagner*

gary**mccord**

*Winner of Senior PGA Tour events
and author of* Golf for Dummies

've never seen a great player yet who doesn't have a good golf brain—that is, a brain that can focus when it needs to focus. Jack Nicklaus focused all the time. Ben Hogan focused twenty-four hours a day. Lee Trevino focused over the shot. But they could all turn it on and get into their certain fog when they needed to.

I had a tendency, if a shot wasn't challenging, to let my mind wander. I could hit a shot better out of the left rough, from underneath a pine tree, cut it up over that other tree, then make it rise another 140 yards over a water hazard, take two spins to the right, and stop.

When I had a 7-iron lay up on a par-5 short of the water, I'd hit it in the water every time. Now I've learned how to get rid of the residual stuff and focus on the shot at hand, play it, and then go do my other stuff.

First, get a club that you know is the right club. Never have a club in your hands that on the downswing you're thinking you need one more club. Next, see the shot. "Okay, the pin's back right and the wind's blowing so I'm going to hit a low cut, low cut, low cut." Just sit there and look at the shot until you see it.

The last thing is to have one key swing thought, whatever it is that week. Those are the three things to go through every shot. Pretty soon all the shots are the same if you prepare for them in the same way.

> ## "So much of the game is played with the heart as well as the mind. It's the combination of both of them."

—Billy Casper, two-time U.S. Open champion, 1959 and 1966

> ## "I get people in my golf school who will hit a solid 2-iron and say, 'That 2-iron feels better than sex.' I tell them, 'You've got to get a new partner. There ain't no 2-iron I've ever hit that's better than sex.'"

—Butch Harmon, founder of the Butch Harmon School of Golf in Las Vegas

tom**sullivan**

Motivational speaker, blind golfer with an 18 handicap

If I were to sum up what my blindness has taught me about golf, and about the mind, I'd say that if you don't have an image of what your goals are, both in terms of emotional and physical issues, you can't play. For example, if you're standing over a shot and you literally cannot picture it in your mind, it's not going to happen. That's the first concept the blind person learns.

The second one is about feeling the game. I am one of the great amateur putters of the world because I don't think about the line in putting. That's the job of my coach, who puts the putter down for me. I relate only to feel. What does it take to move the ball from this spot to that hole? I can read greens with my feet better than sighted caddies can by looking. If you can learn to play the game by using all your senses you'll be a much better golfer.

The third thing is to love the aesthetics. When you play our golf course you can stand on the 4th tee much like you can at Pebble Beach, and hear the ocean, smell the eucalyptus, orange blossom, and lilac, and recognize where the wind's coming from. Some days you can feel the fog coming in and touching your shoulders. All of these sensory things are going on.

What sighted players miss is experiencing the other four senses that make golf wonderful, walking along a fairway and feeling the sponge under your feet; hitting a shot and hearing it go through the trees. I don't mean hitting the trees, but hearing the echo of the shot. It makes you feel like a giant, especially on a par-5, when you're in the middle of the fairway and you hear the well-struck metal wood after you hit it.

You can stand behind a shot and know where you hit it, or where the other guy hit it, by hearing the ball in the air. The "thunk" of a ball coming out of a sand trap is a great sound. The sensory aesthetics of the game are magical, and sighted players don't get those. They don't have the feel that relates to the mental image of the game.

> ## "This business of keeping your head down; so what?"
>
> —*Tom Sullivan*

nancy**haller**

Sports psychologist

Over the years I've found I'm less and less a believer that golf is 100 percent mental. I've discovered it's correlated with skill level. The higher your skill level, the lower your handicap index, the more of a mental game it is.

So if somebody has a 30 handicap, there's some mental ability involved. Stay relaxed, don't get worried that you're the worst in the group, have fun. But for those who are single-digit golfers, the difference between one stroke and the next is really between the ears. Because they have their bodies finely trained, finely honed.

"When you're playing your best and you make a mistake, that doesn't make the tournament. You forget what you did and you press on to what lies ahead. You think of the shot that you're about to prepare for, no matter what you did before."

—Steve Jones, 1996 U.S. Open champion

63

susan**anton**

Stars in a one-woman show in the
Starlight Room of the Desert Inn, Las Vegas

The greatest thing about golf, why I love it and why it's the most precise metaphor for life, is it's so in the moment. It's so in the instant. It's like great acting. You have to know everything about your character. You have to do an in-depth background study to learn what got her to that moment in a particular scene. Then, when it's time to shoot the scene, you have to forget everything and be in the moment, so that it can happen now.

It's not indigenous to human behavior to process ourselves that way. We're always trying to think where we're supposed to be tomorrow or what are we doing next week. Golf will not allow you to be anyplace other than exactly in that moment, and we're not naturally equipped to do that.

When you think about the times you are not thinking about anything, that's when you are living your life in the purest light. It's absolute freedom, because there is no noise. The noise only appears when the ego is engaged, because it's wondering, "How am I doing? How am I looking?" Other people don't care because all they care about is how they're doing and how they look. They don't care that you look like a fool. So why should you care that you look like a fool?

Golf is like the question of life, Why am I here? We will never know the answer. We are determined to think we will figure it out. But we can't. Even someone with incredible talent, like Tiger Woods, can be on the golf course and lose it. All of a sudden, it's gone. If somebody that great can't make it happen every single time, then golf is truly elusive. We somehow think it's something we can get and hold on to and own, but we cannot. However, we can borrow it from moment to moment.

Golf is one of the most dysfunctional relationships a person can ever have. Just when you're about to say, "Forget it. I'm never doing this again," the golf gods let you hole that chip shot, so then you say, "Wait a minute. Maybe I'll stick around."

"The game of golf gets very, very successful people's attention because it's impossible to master. It's the only thing that very successful people can do that they don't have any control over, so it fascinates them."

—*Phil Rodgers, short-game guru*

"I want to use golf as a relaxation from life, not a pressure from life."

—*David Wolper, award-winning movie and television producer*

john**schroeder**

Senior PGA player and television golf commentator

I was never a great player like the guys who focus on the majors. The key for me was to have a constant feeling for my game mechanically. If I felt my mechanics were good then I knew I was going to hit the ball well. I also made sure not to get careless or to try shots I shouldn't try or to let unimportant things bother me. When I did play well, that was my mental state, but if my mechanics were off, it was a fistfight to perform.

If your mechanics are off you play scared. You play defensively because you know you're not up to it. You are much more conservative in your approach to everything. If you are playing well and you have a go at a par-5 and there is water in front of the green, it's no big deal. If you're playing poorly, you're not confident and if you go for it, it's a bad mistake. You just try not to shoot yourself out of the tournament by making bad decisions when you know you aren't physically performing.

The big question is always, Are you willing to take the risk for the reward? That's what makes golf so interesting. If you take a chance and you screw up, you've got to live with it. You've got to say, "Well, I took a chance." What you cannot do is take a risk, miss the shot, and then get mad at yourself. If you decide

67

to take the risk, then you've got to understand the pluses and minuses. That's one side of the equation.

The other side is making the right decision to take a risk. A lot of times I see players who hit shots that are just crazy. I wonder, "Why would he try that shot now? He doesn't have to do that at this stage in the round. It's not that important right at this moment." When it gets down to the last two or three holes and you've got to pull something off, fine. Go for it. But most of the time, aggressive players end up stepping on themselves.

Take Jack Nicklaus. Nicklaus was never real aggressive. He had the best management of anybody on the golf course. He knew his game. He knew what he was capable of and he didn't cost himself shots at critical times when other guys would.

> **"The more out of the ordinary you make a shot, the harder it is to perform."**
>
> —*John Schroeder*

simon**bevan**

Head pro at Glen Abbey Golf Club, Oakland, Ontario

If you don't have the proper mindset in golf, it's very difficult to succeed. It's not like other sports, where natural talent will always prevail, where if you're lacking in some areas, you can make it through. In golf, if you don't have that correct mental approach, no matter how good you are, you're just not going to make it.

We see those other tours, which are loaded with players with talent who are easily as good as the ones on the PGA Tour. But there are a lot of fantastic players who haven't been able to separate the mind from the body.

I don't think anyone would say Hal Sutton is a better ball striker now than he was twenty years ago. He's just making his way around the golf course and using his mind better. Hal Sutton as a kid was the next Nicklaus. But it got to him. His mind took over and he didn't think properly.

Now he's more relaxed, he's more comfortable, and it's showing. I can pretty much guarantee he's not playing better. Ball-striking-wise, I don't think anyone will tell you he's a better ball striker than he was twenty years ago, but he's managed to think better. So there is hope for all of us.

"The hard part about playing golf well is knowing when to hit the accelerator and when to hit the brake. That changes, not round to round, but shot to shot."

—*Hal Sutton, 1983 PGA champion*

"Not every hole is meant to be birdied."

—*Bobby Jones, creator of the Masters*

"The game is simple when you don't get in your own way."

—*Andy North, two-time U.S. Open champion, 1978 and 1985*

tony**gwynn**

Eight-time National League batting champion
with more than three thousand hits

It's a lot easier hitting a baseball than a golf ball because the baseball determines what I do. I take whatever the pitcher gives me and the baseball takes whatever I give it. With a golf ball it's completely different because the ball is sitting on a tee and I'm the one taking the action. I'm more of a counterpuncher than an aggressor, but when I put a golf ball on the tee, all of a sudden I get out of my mode of being a counterpuncher and I become the aggressor. It's especially worrisome with the tee shot.

When I'm in the batter's box, I never really worry about who's on the mound or how hard he throws. I concern myself with seeing the ball come out of his hand. It makes no difference whether he's a right-hander or a left-hander. The sooner I see it come out of his hand, the quicker my mind's going to work to counter where the ball is going and what it's doing so I can get my bat where I need to get it. In the batter's box, I'm pretty calm. On the tee box, I'm anything but calm, because people automatically assume that, as an athlete, I can smoke a golf ball. Well, I can't.

In baseball when I'm in the zone I see the ball as soon as it comes to my sight line. I see it and then I'm able to determine what pitch it is so as a hitter I have more time. It's not that the ball's bigger. It's not that it's slower. It's just that I have more time to determine what it is and where I need to get my bat.

I had this feeling once on the golf course and it was only for nine holes. It was like *Caddyshack*, where the guy was playing the best round of his life. I was playing by myself and I had no witnesses. I was at Mount Woodson where par is 35 and I shot 33. I never brag about it because nobody was there. Nobody saw it. But I was in the zone that day, I got off some great drives and I was on every green in regulation. It was really a lot of fun, but I can't tell anyone about it.

> **"The best advice I've ever received is, 'Let it go.' Just *let it go*. That really helped my golf game. Now I'm not afraid to get over a ball, get a good position, and take a swing. I don't pause, I don't try to guide it, I *just let it go*. I take the swing and wherever the ball ends up, that's where I hit my next shot."**
>
> —*Tony Gwynn*

stan**smith**

1972 Wimbledon, 1969, and 1971
U.S. Open tennis champion with a 6 handicap

In tennis you've got to be able to relax between points and in changeovers without losing your awareness of what's happening around you. You've got to be aware of the wind conditions. You've got to be aware of the sun. You've got to be aware of how your opponent is reacting to different shots, but you also have to be able to relax and perform during the point. Most of the time in tennis there's nothing going on. Most of it is waiting before you play a point, or waiting after a point. Golf is even worse.

The really good golfers have less than seventy swings at the ball. They play for four hours and take seventy swings at the ball. That's about one swing every three and a half minutes, or seventeen swings an hour. So you have to be able to be totally there when you're swinging and then be able to get away from it but still not lose your awareness of what's happening. That's hard to do.

When you're serving in tennis, you have plenty of time to think. But during the rest of the points there are just a few seconds to think about a shot. It's amazing how quickly you can think and change your mind when it's a half volley. You have two or three seconds to think. It's remarkable what you can think about in two or three seconds.

In golf you have three or four minutes to think between shots. That gives you a lot of time to think about bad things. In tennis, within three seconds you can also think about a lot of bad things. It's incredible how you can become very negative very quickly. In both situations you can think about the consequences of not making the shot versus trying to play the shot. However, because you have more time to think in golf, it takes a stronger will to block out negative thoughts and be positive.

"I've forced my players to eliminate the word *can't* from their vocabulary. Instead, I make them say out loud, 'At this point in time, I'm having a difficult time with this shot. However, in the future, it will get better.' Forcing them to say that allows them to go back to the task at hand. All I'm doing is playing tricks on their mind, and these tricks are trying to sweep away the negative thoughts."

—*Dale Walker, golf coach at San Diego State University*

john**brodie**

*Former San Francisco 49ers quarterback
and PGA Senior Tour winner*

'**ve** always felt that there are certain athletes who play better when it gets close. When the game is on the line their ability level improves. That is truer in golf than in anything else. Certain people, under pressure, just get better. That's why you'll see some players shoot lights out when they're in the lead and other players, near the top, will all of a sudden fall off the leader board.

I've always found when I'm playing well that my attention gets keener and I see stuff I never usually see. I don't know why I see it but I do. My viewpoint is, feel comfortable with whatever qualities God gave you and give your best, and recognize that whatever happens, happens. That's the highest level you can achieve.

There are five recent quarterbacks in the National Football League who every time they had to get something done, they did. Aikman, Elway, Marino, Chandler, and Young are just in another league. When I was playing, there were about five of us who were in that league. We knew we were going to get it done. I don't know what it is, but I know that it's true.

"I always wanted to force the outcome, make something happen. Sometimes you have to let events unfold in front of you, and attack when the opportunities are there. It's hard to accept that some things are not in your control."

—*Notah Begay, winner of two Tour titles in 1999, his rookie season*

chapter four

The First Tee

"There are so many
variables that go into
hitting a good golf shot
that you can't possibly
conquer them all."

—Deborah Graham,
sports psychologist

fuzzy**zoeller**

1979 Masters and 1984 U.S. Open champion

What you want to do is picture all good stuff; don't worry about the bad things. The driving range is only to loosen up. I've had some tremendous rounds of golf on days when I hit the ball so poorly on the range that I was embarrassed to be on the golf course. But when I stepped on the first tee I tuned in.

A golf swing is just like dancing. It's a rhythmic move. The rhythm with your wedge is the same as you have with your driver. You want to keep that same rhythm on every swing.

It all comes down to confidence. I learned a long time ago there's no rule in the book that says you have to hit a driver on the first tee. If you don't have confidence in your driver, hit a 3-wood. What you want to do is get in the fairway and get that positive thinking going.

> **"I asked Arnold Palmer if he'd ever come close to mastering the game of golf. He said he thought he had once, for nine holes."**
>
> *—Fuzzy Zoeller*

chris**hoy**

*Head pro at Northview Golf and
Country Club, Surrey, British Columbia*

just finished writing an article for a newspaper, called "The First Tee Jitters." The idea was that players stand on the practice tee and warm up by hitting golf balls. They go from their wedge to their irons to their woods and the last thing they hit is their driver.

They snap-hook four drives in a row, then they walk to the first tee and pull out the driver. Their mind already knows the odds are they're going to fail. Why not pull out the 3-wood?

I use my experience of playing with Arnold Palmer at the opening of our golf course that he designed. He was warming up on one side of the range and there were about four hundred people watching him. I was on the other side warming up because I was nervous, and nobody was watching me.

I'd hit some bad shots with my driver on the range, and on the first tee I looked at my caddie and said, "I should hit a 3-wood here but I'm with Arnold Palmer and you don't do that with Arnold Palmer." Then I thought, "Hang on. I'm allowed to play my game." I pulled out my 3-wood and knocked it right down the middle. The world was so much lighter for me now. I got back on my game plan and I am very proud that I was able to do that while standing next to one of my heroes.

"When you get between those tee blocks, you're not practicing anymore, you're playing."

—*Stan Thirsk, Tom Watson's teaching pro*

"Your driver is the lightest club in your bag, so your grip pressure should be light. You want a lot of club head speed so you can get it to swing fast and you can hit it a long way."

—*Stan Thirsk, head pro at Kansas City Country Club for thirty-two years*

roger**maltbie**

1975 PGA Tour Rookie of the Year
and NBC golf analyst

There's no mumbo jumbo that I can give you that's quick or easy. The most important thing is to develop a pre-shot routine and make that a habit. If you do the same thing over and over in a robotic fashion, your body will have a very difficult time discerning the difference between a pressure situation and being on the driving range. Do your routine every time you hit a ball anywhere. Any shot.

If your routine is to stand behind the ball, pick a spot, walk up behind it, place the club, then your right foot, then your left foot, look at the target, waggle once, look at the target, waggle twice, and swing, you should do that every time in the same cadence.

You literally have to train yourself to do this and it's not easy. Take time on the driving range to merely work on your pre-shot routine, and keep repeating it without caring about where the ball goes. Do it over and over until it becomes habit.

I remember playing with Billy Casper, and his pre-shot routine started when he took the club out of the bag. If he was interrupted for any reason he didn't just back off; the club went back in the bag, and the yardage book came out again. He'd look at that, reach in, grab the club, and start again. Every time. That's how you become robotic. That's really the essence of how you avoid first-tee jitters.

butch**harmon**

Son of 1948 Masters champion Claude Harmon, Sr.

The longest walk in golf is from the practice tee to the first tee. It's all mental because you have just been on the practice tee and physically you've shown yourself you can do it. The difference is that every time you hit a bad shot on the range, you just reach over and get another ball and you hit it.

When you go to the first tee you only get to hit one ball, so what you have to do is prepare yourself mentally for that shot on the first hole. It's not life or death. It's just a golf shot. Go through your normal routine and give yourself a chance to hit a good shot. Only two things can happen in golf: You either hit a good shot or you hit a bad shot.

The average golfer thinks more about hitting a bad shot than he does about hitting a good shot. On the practice tee, he's not thinking any bad thoughts because there are no out-of-bounds stakes, no bunkers, no lakes. He walks to the first tee and gets totally out of his whole frame of thought and concentration. What he should do is go over to the first tee and realize there are only two things that are going to happen. He might as well give himself a 100 percent chance to hit a good shot.

"For the 18-handicap player, his driver swing is not the same as his 8-iron swing. If it was, it would be just fabulous."

—*Simon Bevan, head pro at Glen Abbey Golf Club, Oakland, Ontario*

tom**wilson**

Executive director of the Buick Invitational

When the pros are on the driving range, they are very target-oriented. That's what the majority of amateurs don't do. They don't have a target for every shot. They just hit balls without caring where they go. That's what makes it difficult to take their swing from the practice tee to the first tee. They haven't been aiming at a target.

The other factor in making the transition from the practice tee to the golf course is to specify an actual target off the first tee—a flag, a mound, a trap, or a tree. Too many golfers merely look out at a thirty- or forty-yard-wide fairway and that's their target. It's thirty or forty yards wide.

If they miss the target ten yards one way or the other, they're in the rough. But if they pinpoint a spot in the middle of the fairway as their target and then miss it fifteen yards one way or the other, they have a good chance of still being in the fairway.

"No matter how much you practice, you always tend to put the driving-range swing on it, not the tournament-playable swing."

—Tiger Woods, holds scoring record in all four majors

ken**venturi**

1964 U.S. Open champion and televison golf commentator

You go out and hit fifty golf balls on the practice tee. You hit forty-nine of them absolutely perfect, and then you shank number fifty. Now you go to the first tee and say, "Don't shank it." But wait a minute. What happened to the forty-nine good ones?

Here's what you have to do. I was playing with George Archer and he hit a duck hook off 1, another duck hook off 2, and yet another duck hook off 4. We got to number 6, which was uphill and so narrow you had to walk single-file, and he put it right in the middle of the fairway.

I said to him, "That's amazing!" He said, "What's amazing?" I said, "You've hit three duck hooks and now you hit it right in the middle." His answer: "I haven't duck-hooked in months." Good players have ways of forgetting about their bad shots. They're oblivious.

"Your tee shot on the first hole is important, but only to get you into the flow of your day."

—Peter Jacobsen, founder of the musical group Jake Trout and the Flounders

"On the first tee I want my players to be so nervous that they can hardly control their bladders.
The reason I want them nervous is that after
they hit their first drive, no matter how they hit
it, the nervous sensation and the tension vacate
immediately and they can then focus on the
round and the task at hand."

—Dale Walker, golf coach at San Diego State University

"People are funny. They can be bloodthirsty.
When there are thirty thousand of them waiting
for you at 2 P.M. in Augusta on Sunday at the
Masters, a lot of them are there just to see if you
vomit all the way down the 1st fairway."

—Jackie Burke, Jr., 1956 Masters and 1956 PGA champion

ken**green**

Teaching pro at Aviara Golf Academy, California

There are different ways to get to the first tee. One is to return to your routine so your body knows what it's supposed to do. Another is to practice your first tee shot on the driving range before you get to the first tee. Picture yourself standing there in front of the gallery and go through your routine, so when you get to the first tee, you're thinking about what you're doing. You're not thinking about all the peripheral stuff.

Practice playing golf on the driving range. Play nine holes on the driving range. The reason most people have trouble on the golf course is that the golf course is a totally unique experience because they've never practiced playing golf on the driving range. I guarantee you almost any good player at some point has practiced different holes and played different shots on the driving range.

I used to practice at a driving range that had big oil drums on it. We would hit shots at them. I got so good at it that when I was on the golf course in certain situations, I would mentally put myself back on the driving range and pretend I was hitting it at the oil drum instead of hitting at the flag.

Fred Couples talks about mentally banking shots, which means that every time he has a 9-iron, he's thinking about the perfect 9-iron he hit in the Bay Hill Invitational in 1992. He said that before he hits a shot, he's thinking about a great shot he hit previously with that club. You have to put your mind in the right state to have the expectation or the visualization that you're going to hit a great shot.

glen**daugherty**

Head golf pro at Rancho Santa Fe Farms, California

If I gave you one ball, sent you to the range, and said, "You've got to keep this on the driving range because if you don't, you have to go out there and find it," you'd make the same swing that you would make on the first tee of the golf course.

I've given thousands and thousands of lessons and I hear all the time, "How do I take this swing to the first tee?" The mentality changes because all of a sudden you only have one swing at it. When you're on the range you know that you have three hundred balls sitting there, so you're going to have all these other chances. Then you relax. You figure, "Well, if I don't get this first one, I'll get the next one." You make a more relaxed swing. You relax your muscles, and relaxed muscles work a lot better than tight muscles, especially in a golf swing.

I used to caddie for Phil Rodgers years ago. He would get into a rhythm. He'd hit a lot of balls with his driver and I'd shag for him on the range. Then he'd wave me in and say, "We've got to sit here for about fifteen minutes. I want to see how the next swing goes after I've sat here for fifteen minutes."

On the range you hit shot after shot after shot, and pretty soon you get in an artificial rhythm that you're not allowed to get into on the golf course. There you hit one shot and, hopefully, you have five to six minutes before you hit another shot.

The ideal practice on the driving range is to hit one shot every five minutes. Hit a shot, wait five minutes, hit another shot, wait five minutes. If you want to have a realistic practice don't hit a bunch of 7-irons, a bunch of 5-irons, a bunch of 3-woods, and a bunch of drivers. Hit the driver, wait five minutes, hit the 7-iron, wait five minutes, hit the wedge, then go back to the driver. You'll find your shots will be the same on the range as on the first tee and, hopefully, you'll learn to relax during your individual swings on the driving range. This will lead you to relax on your swing on the first tee.

> **"My strategy is to hit my first drive long and straight and in the fairway, and that will determine the next door I will open."**
>
> —*Hale Irwin, three-time U.S. Open champion,*
> *1974, 1979, and 1990*

dean**reinmuth**

Member of Golf Digest's *professional advisory staff*

Getting to the first tee from the practice tee has to do with the change of environment. It's like you're driving your car down a back road with no other cars and then all of a sudden, you're driving in major freeway traffic with cars zipping in and out all over the place.

What you have to do is realize that there are two different elements. That's the first step. Try not to compare the two, because if you do, you're comparing your golf swing, not the environment problem. You say, "Well, my golf swing fell apart." No, it didn't fall apart, it's just you're not very good at doing it at this level. That's the difference between the amateur and the professional. The professional has become comfortable in the environment of a golf course.

The biggest mistake the average player makes when he practices on the driving range is to think he can hit the same great shots on the golf course. What the Tour player does most of the time is practice. He's only competing a small amount of the time. He goes out and has two practice rounds a week. He doesn't care what his score is.

How many average players play eighteen holes or thirty-six holes a week and don't care what their score is? Almost none. There's the difference. The pros are doing that on each golf course they play, so, including the pro-am, they spend a good part of fourteen hours on these golf courses before they actually compete.

The average player could really help himself if he got into the frame of mind of just hitting shots, getting comfortable, working on his swing, and getting a feel for the golf course itself, such as where to hit it and how to play it.

This is why when you play somebody else's golf course, it's not so easy. You can expect if an average golfer goes to a course he doesn't know, invariably his score will be at least five shots higher, depending on the degree of his ability. It's a putt he reads wrong, it's a distance he missed, it's a tee shot that he's uncomfortable with. That's what it is.

> **"On the first tee we're held prisoner by par. There's this printed number on a scorecard that we're going to be measured by."**
>
> —*Ron Riemer, director of golf equipment advertising for* Golf Magazine

pat**goss**

Golf coach at Northwestern University

We try to be very conscientious of making our players understand that there is practice to make your golf swing better and there is practice to create situations. At Northwestern, we do a lot of what I call technical practice, where we have an isolated period of time when we can't go outdoors because of snow, so we're practicing indoors.

Our goal during that time is to make ourselves physically better players. It's our only opportunity of the year where we're not competing and playing. So we get back to making our golf swings better, making our chipping better, and making our putting better. Then by the end of the week, we need to be able to switch out of that mode and switch into a playing and competition mode.

I want my players to understand when they're practicing that there are times you work on your golf swing and just try to physically improve your game. You don't have much attachment to the results, you have a lot of attachment to what you're building up to. But when it comes time to compete, you better have done some practicing in all situations.

Our players aren't very good when they're on the range in the morning, because they understand their goal at that time isn't to make them better, it's to get them ready to play and to go over some of the situations they're going to encounter on the golf course. They need to be going through their routine, picking different targets, hitting different clubs, just like they would on the first hole.

We'll talk about the first hole that doglegs right to left. It's a 410-yard par-4, with a hazard on the left you have to drive over, and two bunkers on the right. The wind is in and right to left. They need to be able to hit a 3-wood at the bunkers and let it turn a little bit. If anything, their bad shot fans a little bit, they can't pull-hook it.

What we'll do in practice is we'll hit each shot one at a time. I won't let them hit practice shots in between. While you're practicing, as soon as you hit a bad shot, your instinct is to take another ball and, as fast as you can, redo it. That's okay when you're doing certain kinds of practice, but in these situations, you've got to live with what you hit, just like on the course. I want them to walk away like they would in golf, have another three, four, five minutes until they hit another golf shot, and then we come up with another situation.

> **"Every day you have complete accountability for the number that adds up at the end. There's no other sport where that exists."**
>
> —*Pat Goss*

lee**trevino**

Captain of the 1985 U.S. Ryder Cup team

The hardest thing in the world for an amateur to do is go from the practice tee to the first tee. It's hard simply because you don't have to chase your ball on the driving range. Subconsciously you're very comfortable hitting balls there because you know you don't have to retrieve them. Once you get on the golf course, you know you only have that one golf ball and the juices start flowing and you have fear. It's fear that you cannot execute the shot like you do on the driving range.

How many times have you heard people walk to the 3rd hole after they've gone triple bogey, triple bogey and say, "I can't believe this. I never missed a shot on the driving range but I can't hit one here." Amateurs have two different golf games. They have one on the driving range and one on the golf course; that's what separates the pros from the amateurs. We have a game on the driving range and we're able to take it to the golf course.

If the amateur would swing the golf club on the golf course like he does on the driving range, he would be able to take it there too. Most people swing a golf club at the speed of .96 seconds on the golf course. When they get on the driving range, they're a lot slower. They usually swing a golf club at the speed of 1.2 seconds. Then they get on the golf course and the adrenaline starts flowing; they speed up their swing and it's .90 seconds. The reason they do this is that they don't really care how far they hit their driver on the driving range. All they're trying to do is get it off the ground. Once they get on the golf course and the 1st hole is 430 yards, they're trying to hit it 430 yards.

Another thing you should do on the driving range is never hit two shots in the same direction. I've seen players stand there with a wedge and shoot at a one-hundred-yard marker and hit twenty-five balls at it. You might as well put a blindfold on because you've got the line, you've got the feel.

What you need to do is take one ball and hit it to that one-hundred-yard site and then take another ball and move over to the right and swing at something else. Hit the third ball at another marker. With the fourth ball, come back to the one-hundred-yard marker, and with the fifth ball, take it to another place. That way, you are actually realigning yourself with every golf ball you hit. You're aiming at a specific target.

If you really want to learn how to putt, putt with only one ball. You putt and then you have to retrieve it. You have to get it before you can hit another putt. That's how you learn to putt. Once you start hitting more than one ball from the same spot you're wasting your time.

"The hardest thing to teach an amateur
is to slow down their swing."

—*Lee Trevino*

"The first tee is the hardest
shot of the day."

—*John Schroeder, PGA Senior Tour player*

"I call the first tee the grumble tee. 'Geez, I haven't played for two weeks.' 'I have a bad back.' 'My arm is bad.' These are the lines you hear on the first tee."

—*David Wolper, award-winning movie and television producer*

chapter five

The Short Game

"You can't make it happen.
You've got to let it happen."

*—Ken Venturi, 1964 U.S. Open
champion and television
golf commentator*

greg**norman**

*Winner of three Arnold Palmer Awards
and three Vardon Trophies*

The best way to explain the short game is we're trying to lead the ball. If we don't make the shot, we want the ball to finish in the right position where it makes the next shot easier. We're always thinking one shot ahead. For example, if I mishit this shot, where do I want to mis-hit it? Left or right? I'd rather miss it left in the middle of the green than right on the short side of the green. You don't want to think more than one shot ahead because then you are getting out of your game plan.

The same is true with chipping. If you've got a tough little chip, you don't want to try to hit a high lob, a low percentage shot, and leave it in the bunker short side with an even tougher shot. So you always have to think ahead. We play the percentages more than the amateur does.

> **"On the tee, you try to get distance.
> When you get near the hole, you want
> to control the distance."**
>
> —*Dean Reinmuth, member of* Golf Digest*'s
> professioonal advisory staff*

hale**irwin**

Winner of three U. S. Opens and two U. S. Senior Opens

Every time you get to your short game there are two little men sitting on your shoulders. On your left shoulder is the bad guy and on your right shoulder is the good guy. The problem is which one do you listen to?

For most players, the voice of the little bad guy is louder, and he's out-shouting the little good guy on your right shoulder. The bad guy is telling you, "Be careful of this. See that water? See the trap? See that break? You can't do this. You can't do that." He's full of negatives.

The little good guy on your right shoulder is only saying one thing, "See the target?" He's focused on what you need to do. You see it all the time in amateurs. If you give a golfer a one-hundred-yard shot, most amateurs can hit the ball in the air that far. But, if you throw some water in front of them with the same distance, the shot changes. Why? Because they're looking at the water. Rather than see the target, they see the surroundings. The good golfers see the surroundings first and the target last. The last thing in their mind is the first thing they remember, and that's the target.

susan**anton**

Las Vegas headliner and golf fanatic

I don't care how many times I can get out of the sand on the practice range, when I get into a bunker on the golf course I think, "Oh, my God." I don't know why I have such a problem mentally with the sand but I do, and it's a huge problem. However, anytime I have a wedge in my hand, I feel great. I love the pitching wedge and the gap wedge. Anything ninety yards and in, I feel pretty good about.

A wedge is a very manageable club. It's lofted; it's easy to get the ball in flight. You can feel like you know how to hit the ball, so it's easy to build your confidence. It's easy to get the ball on the green. You may not necessarily get it close to the flag, so you may have to spend some time on the putting green, getting yourself into the two-putt zone.

It's like what Tiger Woods' dad did. He started him off with a putter two feet from the hole and worked him back to the tee box. This is the way golf should be taught, because when you think about it, that's where all the strokes really take place. That's where the whole game is played.

For the most part we learn how to play golf in reverse. We want to get out there and really hit it. You see people go to the practice range and the first club they take out is their driver.

They spend the entire time hitting balls with the driver and then when it's time to play they're tired from swinging the most difficult club in the bag. They have nothing left. In addition, they don't know anything else that's going on, including the speed of the greens.

The short game is where even an amateur golfer can really get a small window of insight into the imagination of what the game has to offer. It is like great art. The basics of golf exist but there is an endless world of imagination and execution. Try it this way or try it that way. When you look at what Tiger Woods and Phil Mickelson do around the greens, how they take out their 3-wood and chip, you say, "My God!" This is where you really can begin to be inventive, and this is where you can start to create your own game.

"Somewhere in a round of golf, regardless of our handicap, we'll get to taste greatness. We'll hit one shot as well as Tiger or Phil or Jack."

—*Ron Riemer, director of golf equipment advertising for* Golf Magazine

"It's confidence, confidence, confidence, confidence."

—*Meg Mallon, 1991 LPGA and 1991 U.S. Women's Open champion*

dean**reinmuth**

Member of Golf Digest*'s professional advisory staff*

The most important thing in the short game is to find the distance from the hole where you are so comfortable that you can chip it and get it close. Then start backing up from that point in five-yard increments and keep doing it until you are comfortable at about 50 or 60 yards.

Most people go at the short game with a haphazard approach. They hit a shot and it's 45 yards, the next one's 60 yards, the next one's 25 yards and they think it's a technique issue. If it's a technique issue, you'll find it at 20 yards, and it will be worse at 60 yards. You want to fix it when you're closer to the green, not when you're farther away.

It's a matter of refining how hard you have to swing at the ball. It's like learning how to drive a car. The first thing you do is drive it about five miles an hour with all kinds of safeguards around you. Gradually, you can drive it full speed like everybody else. But you don't jump from the beginning to that speed all at once. Unfortunately, as often as people hear this advice, their response resembles what they say when they're told they need to diet and exercise. They'll say, "What else have you got? I've heard about that and it doesn't work, so what else is there?" The doctor responds, "But did you follow my instructions?" They answer, "No."

tom**sullivan**

Blind golfer with an 18 handicap

I was playing with Fuzzy Zoeller in a pro-am, and we were standing in the middle of the fairway and I said, "Fuzzy, how far do you want me to hit this shot?" He said, "Geez. Hit it fifty yards." I hit it and it was twenty yards short. I said, "Let's walk up there and take a look." We walked and I counted fifty-one steps. I had hit it three feet too far. We're still twenty yards short. I said, "Fuzzy, Jesus. Don't you know distance?" He said, "Yeah. It was a half wedge." I said, "Yeah, a half wedge for you. You can hit it that far." Know your distance, know how far you can fly the ball. I mean, really know it.

"I'm trying to do something that's never been done before. There are blind golfers, but there has never been a golfer who was born blind and tried to learn. The idea that a person who has never seen a golf ball is going to wrap a golf club around his body and then hit that small ball, is asking a lot. I've got a better chance driving a car than hitting this thing. It's a tremendous challenge."

—*Tom Sullivan*

pete**coe**

Head pro at La Jolla Country Club, California

I was giving a golf lesson to a student and he was absolutely the worst player with a wedge I'd ever seen. He hit so far behind the ball that when he got tired he would start to raise up and then he'd scull the ball. He could never, ever hit the ball correctly. It became such a mental block that he got to a point where it was difficult for him to take the club back.

He would make a great practice swing, but once the ball was there, he couldn't hit it. So we started hitting the golf ball with our eyes closed. I would start him off by putting the ball on a tee to make it a little bit easier, and we would hit for an entire lesson. We would hit pitching wedges with our eyes closed. I would do it with him.

If you've never done that before, it is one of the best drills to give you a sense of your balance and where you are in the golf swing. If you don't sense you're ever on your heels or your toes, you certainly will once you've taken a few swings with your eyes closed.

That's why the biggest bunch of baloney anybody's ever said about the golf swing is to keep your head down when you swing the golf club. You do not need to keep your eye on the ball, because you can blindfold yourself and hit the ball just as well. Try it sometime.

bill**roy**

*Head pro at the Country Club of
Green Valley, Arizona*

We learn the short game on the practice green. I'll take players there and have them hit from five yards off the green, then ten, twenty, fifty yards off the green. This ingrains distance in their minds. They can say, "Let's see, when I get on the golf course and I'm five yards off the green, I've got this. Twenty yards, I've got this. I did this on the practice green and I can do this on the golf course." If you can carry that over, it helps a lot. You've got to be thinking all the time.

> **"Golf is a lot of concentration. That's where
> your mind comes into it. You've got to be
> thinking about what you ought to do all the time.
> A lot of concentration and a lot of repetition.
> Over and over. That's what makes a good golfer."**
>
> *—Bill Roy*

annika**sorenstam**

Three-time Vare Trophy winner, 1995, 1996, and 1998

I try to have the same pre-shot routine with my short game. I take as much time as I do on full shots. The visualization there is not so much seeing the ball in the air, it's more of seeing how the ball is going to bounce. Where is the green? Is there slope anywhere?

I grew up loving to hit golf balls. I thought golf was hitting golf balls, but when I came to the U.S. and played college golf and turned professional, I realized the short game is where you save your shots. I believe you can always make up and down from one hundred yards in. Obviously, I don't do it all the time, but I believe in my mind that I can. I believe that with a little patience I can do it. Who cares if you drive it 250 yards if you can't get it up and down from twenty yards?

"So many people try to make golf harder than it is."

—Annika Sorenstam

"Golf is a cruel game. It exposes all your frailties. It attracts us because it gives us a constant challenge to improve. The little accomplishments you get out of it are often so unexpected they are doubly rewarding."

—*Keith Jackson, L.A. Country Club Senior champion and ABC broadcaster*

"Lee Trevino's concentration was that he never stopped talking. If you could ever get him to stop talking, you might beat him."

—*Phil Rodgers, former PGA and Senior PGA Tour player*

"For many years we've seen people without physical gifts who have excelled at golf. How do you explain it if they don't have the gift, if they don't have the raw talent? They just seem to will the ball into the hole. It has to come from within the heart and the mind."

—*Chris Hoy, head pro at Northview Golf and Country Club, Surrey, British Columbia*

butch**harmon**

In 1971, won first B.C. Open on the PGA Tour

The short game is more technique and feel than it is mental. You have to practice your short game because 65 percent of the shots you play during the course of a round are played under one hundred yards—wedge shots, pitch shots, bunker shots, chips, and putts.

Although the average golfer doesn't spend 65 percent of his practice time doing that, the Tour player spends probably 70 percent of his practice time on his short game. The average player just runs out to the tee and wants to hit long drives without paying any attention to his short game. The short game is more technique and not as much mental as the full swing is.

"The short game is such a touch-and-feel part of golf that you need to leave your senses open to feeling what your eyes are telling you."

—Judy Rankin, twice LPGA Player of the Year, 1976 and 1977

chris**hoy**

Head pro at Northview Golf and
Country Club, Surrey, British Columbia

The short game is almost all mind. The three-quarter or the half swing is not something you practice very often, so by the time you're faced with it, your mind immediately says, "I haven't practiced that as much as my full swing. This is going to give me a problem."

Right away you have to adjust your attitude. You have to say to yourself, "I've had quite a bit of success with this shot. I've been able to hit this shot in the past." Maybe you even relate to a shot you hit that was quite spectacular one time. Even if you're really not good with those in-between shots, focus on the one success you remember you had.

The main thing on short shots is to accelerate. Don't take a large backswing and then decelerate into the ball and hit it twenty yards. This seems to be what causes people the most trouble. Just accelerate. Take a shorter backswing and hit through.

ian**baker-finch**

1991 British Open champion

To be very good with your short game you have to be relaxed, you have to feel like everything's easy and within you rather than like you're making a conscious effort. You need to have a positive routine. A positive routine is everything in golf, not just the short game.

When you start thinking, I didn't hit the last one far enough. How hard do I hit this one? or How hard do I hit to get over that hill? you have to give yourself what I call a *toy.* My toy is to say to myself, "Smooth stroke," or "Easy," or "Rhythm," rather than what I tend to say when I get really tense, which is, "Don't miss. Don't screw up. Don't hit it too hard."

It's essential that you remain relaxed and calm, but to do that you have to allow the bad thoughts to pass through and not meddle with your good thoughts. Everyone gets bad thoughts, even the top players. You have to accept that this happens and then move on and concentrate on the things you have done well before, the things you've done well in practice, the simple things.

Under extreme pressure I try to think, Smooth stroke, smooth stroke, smooth stroke, smooth stroke, smooth stroke. Even if I didn't make a smooth stroke, this keeps out the bad thoughts that come into my mind at the wrong time.

If you worry about the lie of the ball, the results, or the outcome, you've got no chance. You have to think simple thoughts such as relax, smooth, rhythm, timing, tempo. Those should be your thoughts as opposed to a conscious effort of thinking, I'm going to hit this ball right at the flag. Players who are good at the short game always look smooth, rhythmical, loose, relaxed, and at ease with themselves. I think that's a big key in the short game, to be loose and relaxed.

> **"Most short game shots are pretty easy,
> if you let them be. You just have to let
> your mind relax."**
>
> —*Mark Loomis, former member of Vanderbilt's golf team*

dale**walker**

Golf coach at San Diego State University

When you're deciding what type of shot to play, you generally want to go with the first thing that comes to your mind. It's very much like taking a test. Whatever pops into your head, so be it. Don't stand there and overanalyze it.

If choking down on a pitching wedge comes into your head, look at the shot and hit it. If you clutter your mind by thinking, Do I want to hit this low? Do I want to hit it high? It doesn't work. Hit the first shot that comes to your mind.

The only way to develop confidence in your short game is to practice. Just go out and practice. Preferably you should practice on the golf course, rather than hitting from the same spot. Go to the golf course, hit a pitch, and then fiddle around with it. That's the only way to develop confidence.

"If your mind is going to work successfully you have to commit to exactly what you are going to do. Once you're totally committed to the kind of shot you're going to hit, you then have to completely specify in your mind what you're trying to do with it. You have got to narrow it down."

—*Pat Goss, golf coach at Northwestern University*

"I've always tried to make all of my swings the same. My 9-iron seems like it swings the same as my driver, only it's just shorter and not as hard."

—*Gene Littler, 1961 U.S. Open champion*

chapter six

Chipping
and Putting

"The closer the putt is, the
more nervous I really get.
I'm thinking, Oh God,
everybody believes I can
make this."

—*Kevin Costner, star of* Tin Cup

butch**harmon**

Founder of the Butch Harmon School of Golf in Las Vegas

When you're putting well, you know you'll never miss another putt. When you're putting poorly, you know you're never going to make another one. It becomes a mental thing, and I don't really have an answer on why that is. Some days you can see it and some days you can't.

Everyone goes through these spells, and you just have to work yourself through them. You have to stay confident. You have to trust the method you're using and eventually you'll work out of the negativeness. Now, that's easy to talk about but it's not easy to do.

The Bob Rotellas and Chuck Hogans of the world have made millions of dollars talking about things that are common sense, because we tend not to think that anything is common sense anymore. It really goes back to the analogy, and I use this all the time, when you putt you can only do two things: You can make it or you can miss it.

You might as well give yourself a positive chance to make the putt. Trust the line you've picked, commit yourself to that line, and just make a stroke. After you've hit it you're at the mercy of the green. There are some days you hit bad putts and they go in, and some days you hit good ones and they don't go in.

After a three-putt you have to tell yourself, "I can't go back and hit it again. Let's see if I can do something else here." It's common sense. Once you've three-putted, you've three-putted. One thing about golf is you can't go back and erase your past. It's done. You might as well go to the next shot or the next green with a positive thought.

However, if you're a bad putter, you can have all the positive thoughts you want and you still won't be any good. I'd recommend you get a halfway decent stroke and put a little work on your mechanics. You can be the most positive person in the world, but if you can't putt, you can't putt.

I love Jackie Burke's analogy of teaching a beginner. He takes him to the putting green and has him putt from three feet for about an hour. The beginner finally says, "Mr. Burke, are we ever going to hit any balls?" And Jackie answers, "Not if you can't make it from here. It won't do you any good to hit any."

> ## "The scariest words in all of golf are, 'It's a straight putt.'"
>
> *—Bill Murray, author of* Cinderella Story

> ## "The biggest thing we fight in golf is tension. You have to let the body perform what it's supposed to do."
>
> *—Ken Green, teaching pro at Aviara Golf Academy, California*

billy**casper**

1970 Masters and two-time U.S. Open champion, 1959 and 1966

The driver and the putter are the two most important clubs in your bag. The driver consumes 60 percent to 80 percent of the distance on every hole. The putter is the one club that can save you. I worked hard on my putting. I was too lazy to go out and hit golf balls on the range, so I spent a lot of time around the greens and in the sand. I developed an extremely sound short game.

When I caddied, several of us would putt in the dark after everybody had gone home. I really think that's where I developed my feel for putting, by putting in the dark. It was a psychological thing. We would walk up to where we could see the hole, implant that in our subconscious, then go back and putt. Quite often we would knock them all very close to the hole. We couldn't see the impurities on the green, so we just concentrated on making a good stroke.

I never, ever thought I could make them all. On any long putt, I always tried to putt it within a two-foot circle of the hole. It didn't make any difference whether it was short or to the right, or whether it was long. I wasn't a bold putter. I was more of a putter who put the ball on the line and let it die next to the hole. I made my share of those putts because of my ability to read the greens as well as my touch and feel.

gary**m^ccord**

PGA Senior Tour winner and television golf analyst

In putting, distance is everything. You have to learn to hit the fifteen-foot putt sixteen feet, and the thirty-foot putt thirty-one feet. Until you can get the ball by the hole, ten to fourteen inches every time, you're not going to be a good putter.

If you do that and if your mechanics are good, putting is ethereal. You go in and out of consciousness all the time, with the feeling that the ball absolutely looks like it is so small, and the hole is so big, that no living idiot could ever miss it. Then there are times when the ball looks bigger than the hole, and it won't fit.

You have to get back into the goodness and not the badness of putting. Otherwise you just take your oar and throw it in the ocean. Putting is the one thing that is delicate in this game. It is putting that affects the psyche.

"If there's a key to being a good putter it's having a deep understanding of how to hit the ball squarely."

—Paul Runyon, two-time PGA champion, 1934 and 1938

gene**littler**

Winner of the 1954 San Diego Open as an amateur

Putting is where confidence comes in, big time. If you don't think you're going to make it, you're probably not going to. As some players get older you can see they have a problem with putting. Ben Hogan is a great example; he couldn't even take the putter back, and he could still play!

The last time I played with him was in Fort Worth, and he'd have a two-footer and he'd stand there and stand there and stand there. It was agonizing because he couldn't take the putter back. Then he'd finally say, "Aw. Pfff. The heck with it." He'd make a quick stab at it and miss. But when he had a thirty-footer, he'd put a nice stroke on it. That *has* to be mental. It's the fear of missing something you're supposed to make.

It's not easy to accept but you have to realize you're going to make some and you're going to miss some. In my first year on the Tour, I was playing with Jackie Burke, who would go on to win the Masters and the PGA. I was really grinding, trying to shoot a score, and I was fretting. Jackie pulled me aside after the round and said, "Look, you can only do two things with a putt. You're either going to miss it or you're going to make it. Go ahead and give it a stroke." He thought I was just grinding too hard and locking up.

I tried to keep Jackie's attitude. It's good because what else can you do? Go ahead and hit it. You're either going to miss it or make it, and if you just keep rolling it toward the hole, some are going to go in and some aren't. You have to realize it's a percentage game. The more you hit at the hole, the more are going to go in. You just have to accept that some days they do and some days they don't.

> ### "Wasn't it Ben Hogan who said, 'Putting shouldn't even be a part of the game'?"
>
> —*Chris Hoy, head pro at Northview Golf and Country Club, Surrey, British Columbia*

> ### "Putting is the same way for us as it is with the amateurs. There are days that hole looks like a damn bucket and other days, it looks like a thimble."
>
> —*Fuzzy Zoeller, 1979 Masters and 1984 U.S. Open champion*

greg**norman**

Winner of three Vardon Trophies, 1988, 1989, and 1994

The mind has a greater effect on your putting stroke than anything else. The putting stroke is the simplest action of the lot, but it really comes from pure confidence. We golfers have a tendency to overcomplicate our putts, from the apex to the speed. We ask ourselves, "Are we trying to make it? Are we not trying to make it? Are we making this for a double bogey? Are we making this for an eagle?" We'll also say, "We have to make this to pull within two shots of the leader," or "We have to make this to pull ahead of the leader."

Basically, all you have to do is think about hitting a solid putt. Think of that one thing and only that one thing all of the time. However, what usually happens is you have all these ancillary things flying into your mind because when you're putting, you are just standing around watching other people putt and you have a lot of dead time.

Normally, when you are hitting shots and walking down the fairway, you are taking in a lot of other things because you are walking and moving, but when you are standing dead still, that's when you have a tendency of mentally drifting and losing your focus.

chris**hoy**

*Head pro at Northview Golf and
Country Club, Surrey, British Columbia*

When you hit your putt, do you see it going into the hole? If it's a straight putt it's going to go over the hole, it's going to hit the back of the cup and fall to the bottom. You're going to hit it with some aggression to make sure the ball gets to the hole. You're not going to let it topple over the front edge.

If it's a breaking putt, it might come in from the side, so there's no use looking at the front of the hole. You have to look at the entry point, and it has to go into the hole with a little bit of speed. Once you have decided how you are going to putt, you can then putt better, because now you have fewer things going through your mind.

When you make a decision on how you're going to putt, go ahead and do it. Even if it misses the hole, you win, because you've succeeded in doing what you decided to do. I don't mind missing if I acted on my decision. What I hate is being indecisive and changing my mind in the middle of the stroke, regardless of whether it's a drive, a wedge, or a putt. I don't want my mind taking over. *I* want to decide.

It keeps coming back to attitude. You have to possess a successful attitude and say, "I'm going to do it."

annika**sorenstam**

Won a record eighteen LPGA tournaments in the 1990s

Pretend you're the ball and think, "Where do I need to go to get to the hole?" Speed is very important. A lot of golfers, when they have a long putt or long chip, think only about the line. "I need to hit it three feet right or twenty feet left." But it's the speed that is so important and that's where fear comes in. You'll say to yourself, "Don't hit it too hard."

I try to prepare before it's my time to putt. When it's my turn I put the ball down and look at the line and putt. I always pay attention to other players' putts, not their strokes. If they have a long putt you can learn from their line. So always look around.

I also go above the hole to read a putt. Probably 90 percent of the time I go to the other side. But if it's a big breaking putt, I always go on the low side; I never go on the high side and look. I always want to see the break from the low side. When I look from the side I'm putting from, I try to pay attention to the first third. When I look from the other side, I pay attention to the last third.

wally**goodwin**

Former Stanford University golf coach

I may be the only guy who's going to tell you this: You can't chip from the fringe unless you've chipped from the fringe a million times. You can't hit wedge shots to the green near the pin unless you've hit a million. You need to know exactly what club and what swing gets the ball a certain distance in the air. The only way you'll ever figure out those shots is to practice them a lot.

The mind is involved, but it's also the physical feeling of confidence knowing that you've done it millions and millions of times. We used to putt four- and five-foot putts by the hour, just so the guys could say, "I've hit a million of these." If you haven't hit a million of them, if there's any question in your mind of not being able to read the break or feel the speed, then it's going to be luck. It's not going to be anything else but luck.

If you hit them a lot, your mind knows you've hit them a lot, so your mind takes over. There is a great serenity in knowing that you've done a certain thing lots and lots of times; therefore, you should be able to do it again.

julie**murphy**

Golf Magazine *account manager and a 14 handicap*

Putting is all in the mind. You have to think that the ball is going to go in the hole. There are days when I can't get near the hole. I can't do it. There are other days when I just look down and know, "This ball is going in."

If it's thirty feet away, my playing partners will think, "She'll never make it." But I step up, take the read, and know it's going in. That's the power of the mind. There are some days when you have it and some days when you don't. I have no idea how one maintains that feeling of absolute certainty. It's a mental puzzle.

> **"I play really fast. I want to get up there and not think about my shot."**
>
> —*Julie Murphy*

"The most important part of putting is trying to stay positive and trust your stroke."

—*Scott Simpson, 1987 U.S. Open champion*

"You've got to stand over every putt with the intent that you're trying to make it. If you're not going to try to make it, then why bother to hit it?"

—*Ken Green, teaching pro at Aviara Golf Academy, California*

ken**venturi**

1964 U.S. Open champion and television golf commentator

At the California Golf Club, we had a huge, huge putting green that had a hedge around it. When it was a foggy, windy, cold day, I'd get next to this hedge and I'd dump my balls on the side of the putting green. I'd take out a 6-iron, and I would chip and chip and chip.

I would never chip to the same hole twice. I'd chip to number 6. I'd chip to number 9. I'd chip to number 18. I'd chip to number 4. I kept chipping to every different hole. I was feeding my eye and my hand into the computer. My eye said, "It's that far," and my hand said, "This is where you have to chip it."

You should never just chip to the same hole ten, fifteen, or twenty times because it doesn't register. You should chip to different holes because you're feeding that information into the computer. As soon as your eyes see that distance, they tell your hands, "This is how hard you have to hit it."

I do clinics today and I can still say, "This one will go here and this one will go there, and now I'll put this one right to the back edge of the green." It'll go within six inches of the back edge, because my eyes say to my hands, "This is how hard you hit it."

ellie**glaser**

The chipping and putting mindset is, there's no room for error. When I was in college I was not the longest hitter on the University of Miami team but I was the most consistent player. I knew that every time I played I was going to be within two or three strokes of my game, regardless of what course I was on.

Some girls were hitting it 280 yards off the tee and I might have been hitting it 230. They might have been fifty yards in front of me, but when I got close to the green I knew that I was going to get it there. Chipping and putting levels the playing field and makes everybody equal. Whoever masters that part of her game, on that particular day, is going to win.

The key to good putting is good practice. Practice from short distances, have fun with the long distance. If you practice and have confidence that everything from ten feet is going in, it's amazing how many chips and putts start to drop. You stop leaving it short. It's so aggravating to leave it short.

bill**roy**

Head pro at the Country Club of Green Valley, Arizona

In putting you have to visualize a three-foot circle where the cup is. A lot of people think this is an old wives' tale, but it's not, because if you can get within that three-foot circle when you're on the golf course, the first thing you're going to do is eliminate the three-putts.

If you look at your scorecard when you come in you'll say, "God, I only had one three-putt green." If you have a twenty-five-foot putt, don't feel as if you're going to sink it. Get it close. Get it close to eliminate that three-putt. It goes back to concentration and the mind.

> **"Where the mind is so important in putting is believing in your ability to control the distance the golf ball goes."**
>
> —*Pat Goss, golf coach at Northwestern University*

"Because I thought my putter was technically working, I became a better putter. I put a better stroke on the ball. I got it into my mind that the tool was better. Once that happened I believed it, I relaxed, and relaxation is the key. I became more able to trust my mind."

—*Mike Spacciapolli, vice chairman of Carbite Golf*

"You can be a good putter and make a lot of putts, but can you do it when you need to do it on Sunday to win a tournament? There's a difference."

—*David Duval, winner of the 1997 Tour Championship*

ben**crenshaw**

Two-time Masters champion, 1984 and 1995

The secret to putting is to trust your judgment before you hit. You have to have an idea of what the ball's going to do. But the method is no different. It's a solid strike. The more times you hit the ball solidly, the more times you're going to putt better than if you hit the ball all over the putter face.

I try to play the highest line I can because I think that's the safest way I can putt. I play all putts to die at the hole. However, on an approach putt, I'll try to bring the ball in high and soft so it won't get away from the hole that much. I think most people who three-putt hit the ball on a lower line and with the wrong speed. That's why I hit it very high and soft. I just try to get the ball close so I can tap in the next one.

"Good putters believe they are good putters."

—Curtis Strange, five-time Ryder Cup team member

lee**trevino**

*First player in U.S. Open history to play in
all four rounds in the sixties, 1968*

Don't blame the putter so much. A lot of guys go right into the pro shop and buy another putter. We have an old saying on Tour that when we're putting poorly, we go get another putter, but it doesn't take that putter long to know who has it. Once it gets to know you, it will start putting just like the one you threw away.

A lot of three-putts happen because players start looking up. They anticipate the hit. I do it. Not all the time, but I'm guilty of it. To stop looking up on your putts, listen for them to go in. Pretend your ball is on a coin and when you putt the ball from the top of the coin, see if you can tell me the date of that coin before you look up to see where the ball went. Keep your head down and listen for the ball to go in.

Gary Player is the best at that I've ever seen. He'll listen for a thirty-footer. I've played with him and I'll say, "Okay, Gary, you can look up now, you left it short." Once the ball is gone and the putter is out of your vision, look down at the coin another split second and then look up to see where the ball is going. People look up too much. That's how three-putts happen.

kevin**sorbo**

Television star of Hercules:
The Legendary Journeys *and an 8 handicap*

I t was probably ten or twelve years ago when Jack Nicklaus took a triple bogey at the Masters and then went birdie, birdie, birdie right after that. I just said, "Wow." You could almost see his mindset.

When I moved to Hollywood I worked my butt off to get to where I am today, and I have that same mindset. If I want something bad enough, I'm going to get it. It was a great lesson for me to watch Nicklaus's mindset. He said, "Okay, I had a bad hole but now I'm back. I'm even par for the last four holes." He could have been mad about it and gone bogey, bogey, bogey and walked home.

That once happened to me on the set. We were losing light and we had one last chance to shoot a scene that had three pages of dialogue. I was going crazy. My brain was saying, "This is impossible." The director said, "Action." Boom. I just did it.

Something happens to me when the director says, "Action," and I think the same thing happens to the guys who are golf pros. It happens when they say their own, "Action." It's not about money. It's all about competition and the win. Even my golfing buddies feel that way. It's not the dollar nassau. It's all about the win.

"Your best reads on the green are usually from behind the ball to the hole. Sometimes we're just walking around trying to steady our nerves."

—*Scott Simpson, 1988 Buick Invitational champion*

"I think good putters see the ball going in; bad putters see the ball staying out. When I'm positive, I see it going in. When I'm negative I take that week off."

—*Chi Chi Rodriguez, winner of the Ambassador of Golf Award in 1981*

chapter**seven**

Visualization

"Visualization is the
biggest key, seeing the
shot before you hit it and
merely letting yourself
do it."

—*Scott Simpson, 1987*
U.S. Open champion

nancy**haller**

Sports psychologist

The more I work with athletes, the more powerful I find visualization, how one can go back and re-create emotions and images. What this means is even if you haven't performed well, you can correct it under imagery. I use visualization, imagery, and hypnosis almost interchangeably. To me, they create almost the same alpha waves you're making in the brain. These techniques are very powerful if people are not frightened of them and if they feel safe.

> **"Jack Nicklaus visualized every shot of the round before he went off to play."**
>
> —*Glen Daugherty, head golf pro at Rancho Santa Fe Farms, California*

glen**daugherty**

Head golf pro at Rancho Santa Fe Farms, California

The great golfers have the best imaginations. They imagine themselves playing great golf all the time and they imagine the shots. They call it visualization. I call it imagination. Tiger Woods, for example, looks at shots people think are unplayable and he invents something. He imagines the ball going in the hole. The shots he pulls off seem impossible. He stands with his feet spread five feet apart and takes a big, giant swing at the ball. The ball pops up and down like a lob shot. He just can't imagine anything but success.

Tiger's swing obviously has awesome power, and his mechanics are good. But there are guys with swings as good or better than his. So you have to say, "What makes Tiger, Tiger?" Another great example is, "What made Nicklaus, Nicklaus?" It's the fact that they are always visualizing, imagining themselves doing all these things successfully. They only imagine themselves winning. They only think about winning and they really believe that the first spot is reserved for them, unless they make a mistake.

"The most important part of my game is that I want to be the best. I won't accept anything less than that."

—*Jack Nicklaus, winner of seventy PGA Tour titles*

pete**coe**

Head pro at La Jolla Country Club, California

I'm an extremely confident putter and always have been. I don't even think about it. Once I line up the putt and start walking to it I see an image of the ball rolling into the hole. It's a continuous picture of the ball rolling into the hole, and that's all I ever see. As I'm looking from the ball to the hole, I see the ball rolling toward the hole and going in. The most important thing for me has always been seeing this never-ending videotape of the ball going into the hole.

What that does is keeps me focused. If I don't do that, my mind tends to drift into some other part of the stroke, or I start to second-guess the break of the putt. It keeps all those thoughts out of my mind. Visualization has been very, very effective for me and I use it a lot in instruction.

"I close my eyes and see the shot. I look at the ball and see the type of shot I have in my mind. I see it fly and then I see it land. It's a way of seeing the result before you do it. I visualize the end result."

—*Annika Sorenstam, two-time U.S. Women's Open champion, 1995 and 1996*

"You need a creative mind. You have to be able to visualize the different shots. You have to make it happen."

—*Tommy Jacobs, runner-up in the 1964 U.S. Open and the 1966 Masters*

"Golf is all about calm. You don't play golf to relax, you relax to play golf. The zone we hear PGA Tour players talk about is a metabolic state of calm, a Zenlike concentration."

—*Gary Haykin, golf teacher and acupuncturist*

tom**sullivan**

Actor, motivational speaker, and golfer with an 18 handicap

I've been blind since birth, but I can still visualize. First of all, since I can hear the ball in the air when it's hit, the visuals I draw are from hearing the flight of the ball and feeling that marvelous impact when you know you've hit it flush. The pros always talk about it going through butter. Well, I'm looking for that butter feel. If the shot flies two hundred yards, I'm picturing what that really means if I were to walk two hundred yards. I reinforce the pride you feel in the game when it goes where you aim it.

I visualize distance. I visualize contact. I visualize the aesthetics of the joy I'm going to feel when I hit it well and then walk down the fairway. I'm aware of all the sensory stuff that's going on. My pictures are all about optimism. I'm trying to draw a picture that says, "This is going to be wonderful." If it sucks, it sucks, but the picture I'm drawing is, "This is going to be wonderful. I'm going to love this shot."

With the driver, I picture the club coming back with a full shoulder turn. I picture a sweeping motion. Whereas when I'm hitting a pitching wedge, I try to play the ball back and hit down. The other thing about blind golf is I try to reduce moving parts as much as possible. With the exception of the driver,

I try to take a three-quarter swing and try to control where the club's going.

In my case, I've got to be very club-head conscious, because it's easy for a blind person to fall. Since I don't have to look at the ball, it's easy for me to get in the habit of sliding or turning too much, or doing things that from a body mechanics standpoint aren't good. I have to have a very, very, very economical golf swing, except with the driver, which I allow myself the pleasure of hitting the shit out of.

"One of the fun parts of the game for me is that every single person who I've ever played with has tried to give me a lesson. Even if they're a 35 handicap! It's like, 'The poor blind bastard, let's teach him something.' I get it all the time."

—Tom Sullivan

bill**ogden**

*Head pro at North Shore Country Club
in Chicago for forty years*

Being able to visualize the shot starts with the mind, as does being able to concentrate. Those are important things. Self-hypnosis is also helpful. Hypnosis involves relaxation and concentration. For instance, when Arnold Palmer was really good, you could go up to him and you could just see that his eyes were transfixed. He was in such a state of concentration that he hardly recognized his wife, Winnie. Some call it the zone. You can call it what you want. It is so important for a good golfer to be in that hypnotic state. Great players definitely have the ability to put themselves into that zone.

A lot of people are naturally able to do it. Others have to learn it by going to a sports psychologist or by learning to hypnotize themselves. I learned how to do it when I was a young teenager. I played very well in amateur golf, and I would get into that state naturally. Then I lost it. I had to reacquire it. Others have to do the same thing.

"When you're in the hunt you always have
to see good shots. You have to see only
positive things."

—*Tommy Jacobs, member of the 1965 U.S. Ryder Cup team*

dean**reinmuth**

Member of Golf Digest*'s professional advisory staff*

If a person doesn't know how to hit a shot, visualizing that shot isn't going to teach his body how to do it. If you sit down and visualize being a pianist, but you don't play the piano, you're not going to be a piano player just by visualizing how to do it.

There is a certain amount you can start to pick up, and your eyes can be a factor in seeing things. But you can't mistake that for the fact that you physically must learn how to become aware of what your body is doing while you're doing it and relate that to a general picture.

After you've done that and you can hit some shots, your brain says, "If I do this, the ball does that." You can then go out and say, "I need the ball to do this," and the brain kicks into a reverse mode and tells your body, "If you need to do that, it feels like this." But this will come and go.

There are times when it's very strong and there are times when you just can't find it. That's when you have to go with something more manual to get you through until it kicks back in gear again. You have to have a fallback position, which is why you'll see players hit certain shots, the ones they're the most comfortable with, in pressure situations.

deborah**graham**

Sports psychologist

The PGA Tour used to have qualifying school at Sawgrass. I had a player who was on the 17th tee, the par-3 island green. He hit the shot into the water and ended up not getting his card, missing by one stroke. He was so upset that he replayed that shot over and over in his mind. He finally did get his card and he played well enough to get into THE PLAYERS Championship at Sawgrass several years in a row. But guess what happened every single time he hit the ball on 17? He put it in the water. Every single time.

We started working with him on Tuesday afternoon of the championship and we had him use the imagery he wanted on that shot. He had two days before the tournament to reprogram. He used positive images, imagining himself staying really relaxed, imagining that long walk from 16 to 17, imagining himself staying with his pre-shot routine.

His only goal was to do his routine well. Guess what he did? He made par. He didn't birdie it but he made par on the 17th hole all four days of the tournament. That's how powerful the mind is. If you don't go back and reprogram a little bit, it can haunt you. You can have memories that stay in your mind forever on holes, but it's possible to change them fairly quickly if you will do the right things.

ron**riemer**

Director of golf equipment advertising for Golf Magazine

This story goes back to the 1970s. The scene is Shoal Creek, the site of Lee Trevino's victory in the PGA Championship. Chuck Hogan was working with Raymond Floyd, who has an interesting ability to see things in great detail. If you were sitting in a restaurant with him and a man was walking a dog outside, everyone at the table would look and then turn back and have some conversation about the dog.

In reality, you and I might have seen the dog right away, which is normal for people. With Raymond Floyd there was a little time lag, like half a second, where he would see nothing. But when he finally saw the dog, he would see a different dog than you and I. He'd say, "Yeah, that was an interesting dog. It must have been in a fight as a puppy, because it had a little notch out of the corner of his left ear."

Because Raymond sees in such detail, he has to be concerned about looking too long at a putt. He sees yesterday's spike marks. He overthinks the putt when he really needs to react very quickly.

At one point, Raymond's mental imagery was to look at his golf ball and then look at the hole and visualize a train, a locomotive, taking his ball on railroad tracks and dropping it into the cup. Those tracks would stay there in his mind's eye. One time Raymond went to put his ball back down after going through his visualization techniques, and he had to re-mark it and step away. He was getting nauseous because when he got down by the ball, the fumes from the locomotive were still there. That's how vivid his imaging is.

I can relate to this because ot something that has happened to me on three occasions. I have marked my ball on the green, cleaned it, and put it in my pocket because I like to have both hands free. It was now my turn to putt. I came back over the ball after completing all my visualization techniques, and I was in my pre-shot routine. I'd taken my two practice swings, stepped over the ball, placed my putter head behind the ball, taken my one final look at the hole, brought my eyes back and took the putter blade back, but there was no ball there. The ball was still in my pocket. My visualization had been so intense that I had mentally placed the ball on the green. Everybody laughed at me because they just thought I was fooling around when, in fact, I was dead serious. I had taken the putter back to hit the ball when there was no ball there.

When I was really cranking with the mental side, I would visualize lighting my ball on fire, rolling this flaming ball into the hole, and then seeing that charred line. I could see it as if it was there, painted with a paintbrush. You can't tell me that the line wasn't there. All I had to do was hit my ball on it and it would go in. To me, this truly demonstrates the mental side of golf.

stan**thirsk**

Tom Watson's longtime teaching pro

You should go out and walk the course backward. Start at the 18th green and then look back at the tee. You'd find a hole that is totally different from what it looks like when you're standing on the tee.

If you start at the back of the green and then walk to the tee, you'll find that sometimes those fairways are a lot wider than you think. Why? Because the architect put bunkers, water, and trees out there to scare you, to make you tense, and to put fear in you.

If you are a high handicapper, par for you is a bogey—a 6, not a 5. Play your game to make sure you do that, and most of the time you'll come out pretty good. You'll save a lot of strokes, win a lot of $2 Nassaus, and have bragging rights. For players who typically shoot 90, winning two dollars is as exciting for them as what we see the pros do on television. It's the same; it's just different numbers.

"I think of myself as an eternal optimist. All I need is a little shred of evidence and I go crazy. It's not reality that's important, it's what we think we are."

—*Shelly Hamlin, 1992 LPGA Bounceback Player of the Year*

butch**harmon**

Teacher of Tiger Woods,
Greg Norman, and Davis Love III

One of the things that sets Tiger Woods apart from other players is his creativity and his imagination, and that's what trouble shots are all about. You have to visualize the shot, try to create the curvature of the spin and the trajectory of the ball, and then go ahead and commit to what you see by doing it.

Some people are very creative and have the ability to see a shot. Other people can't. We could put two players in the rough, and one player would see four different shots he could hit out of there—around something, over something, under something, in between something. The other player wouldn't see any of them and he would just chip out.

We practice trouble shots all the time with Tiger. We do it around the green and out on the course. I'll put balls in terrible positions and say, "What would you do? Let me see what you'd do here." I always add, "Show me what you've got. You're supposed to be the greatest player in the world. What can you do with this?"

Tiger will then hit it two or three different ways. The only way to be creative is to just do it. You can stand on a wide open practice tee without a tree in front of you and get creative. You can hit your shot around one flagpole to another, hit it way over to the left, or way over to the right. All of this practice will help develop your creativity and imagination.

> ### "The biggest strength of Tiger Woods you can't see. It's his mind."
>
> —*Butch Harmon*

> ### "I don't believe I ever played a shot that I didn't visualize first."
>
> —*Ken Venturi, 1964 U.S Open champion and television golf commentator*

"If you cannot visualize, that's a clue to relax
and get the picture in your mind before you take
the shot. Otherwise, you're setting yourself up
for failure. If you can't see it, don't hit it."

—*Deborah Graham, sports psychologist*

chapter eight

When Disaster Strikes

"Disaster is a very
common thing on the golf
course. You've just got to
learn to deal with it."

*—Annika Sorenstam, who has
qualified for induction in the
LPGA Hall of Fame*

gary**mccord**

PGA Senior Tour winner and television golf anaylst

All we're doing out here on the Tour is managing our golf ball. Some days we have better technique than other days, but it's just managing our ball around the golf course. You learn after a while there are going to be certain days you haven't got it. But, if your management skills are good, you can figure out a way to get around the golf course in a way that the wounds are only superficial. You go from an offensive mode to a defensive mode to get you through the day.

Basically, it comes down to the evolution of the species. The faster you can evolve, the better, which means if I have swing problems, I can't call my swing doctor and wait to fix it after two weeks at his golf course. It's too late. I have to get it done before the next shot.

I have to understand the complexities of my golf swing, my technique. If I'm pulling it, what's the reason? I have to analyze it quickly. It's no time to dawdle and say, "Oh, I can't wait to get to my guru so he can figure it out." You have to figure it out yourself. I think players on the Tour are very aware of their swing tendencies and how to correct them immediately, because the one who can correct his swing the fastest is going to evolve higher in the species.

johnny**miller**

First player elected to the World Golf Hall of Fame

I used to get a kick out of being in the last group or two so I could watch the players to see if they started arguing with their caddies. Were they irritable, did they take five or more waggles, or did they start hearing the grass grow? I liked to see if they got stressed out and if the wheels would start falling off.

I did that for fifteen years of my career. I almost received my doctorate in watching players basically choke. I always say choking is when you hit a duck hook off the tee and you haven't duck-hooked in six months.

My disaster came at Pebble Beach when I shanked one in my first Bing Crosby tournament. I had a chance to win. I was tied with Jack Nicklaus and it's still the most famous shot I ever hit. I was on the 16th and I had a little downhill lie. I thought, Well, I'll do my little Tony Lema knee-action graceful thing, and I shanked it right up against a tree. I chipped it out into the bunker and almost holed the bunker shot.

Nicklaus three-putted the next hole but nobody remembers his bogey. All they remember is my shank. I'd never hit that shot before, so obviously, I must have been a little nervous. That's my definition of gagging. By the way, Jack birdied the first extra hole to win.

chip**beck**

Tragedy is always a part of golf. It's kind of nice you can experience tragedy and not get hurt. You always experience tragedy in life, no matter what. It makes you persevere. It makes you stronger. That's the part that really trains you. It's even biblical. You have the trials that lead to that perseverance, which leads to hope, so it strengthens your character because you realize you have to do it yourself. You have to pick yourself up and be the one who keeps yourself going.

"Golf is an individual sport. You're the judge, the jury, and you're the one going to prison. You're the one who has to make all the decisions."

—Lee Trevino, winner of twenty-seven PGA Tour victories,
including six majors

ian**baker-finch**

*Winner of events in Australia, Japan, America, and
Europe, including the 1991 British Open*

If you really focus on the problem, if you really focus on trying to fix something, you're focusing on a negative, and you become more and more negative. To overcome adversity you must focus on the positive. Think about the five shots you hit well near the end of the round, rather than the one that gave you the double-bogey at the last hole.

Personally, I was trying to fix something and I didn't even know what I was trying to fix. I was just focusing on the outcome all the time, trying to fix my swing or fix my mind. It got so bad that I was focusing on negatives all the time, and it drained me. I just felt like there was nothing left.

I now know you need to go out, relax, and really try hard at trying less. If it's not easy, you're not doing it the right way. You still need to practice, to do your sit-ups and push-ups, and hit thousands of balls. I'm not saying you get away with it just because you have a good mind. But, if you're thinking about fixing a problem, then you're focusing on the negatives rather than focusing on the positives. Go out and trust yourself. Trust is a must.

You've got to see the shot and play in a relaxed frame of mind. There's the ball, there's the hole, get the ball in the hole in as few shots as possible. You must also remember that at the end of the day, it is only a game. It may be your livelihood as a golf professional, but one shot, or one hole, or one round, or one week, or one year isn't going to change your life to the extent that it really matters that much.

> **"It's just the way golf is sometimes. You can go out and play beautifully, and a couple of shots later you can't find it."**
>
> —*Tiger Woods, first player to win three consecutive U.S. Men's Amateur Championships, 1994, 1995, and 1996*

stan**thirsk**

Head pro at Kansas City Country Club for thirty-two years

When disaster strikes, you're going to have an anxiety attack. Take a deep breath and back off. The first thing you need to do is to take a little practice swing and get yourself under control, see if you can really feel the weight in that club head as you swing it. If you cannot feel it, then that's probably why things are not going too well. You'd better back off and get your grip pressure down so you can feel what you're doing again.

Tom Watson has a little drill. He turns the club over and holds the club head in his hands, swings the grip end, and makes the club swish at the bottom. If he can't make that swish down at the bottom, this tells him he's putting too much pressure on the handle end of the club. What's that going to do to the club face in the swing path? The club head is going to change and so his ball is going to go places he doesn't want.

"A lot of touring pros use rhythmic breathing to help quiet their nerves. They'll use breathing techniques as they walk down the fairway. Take a series of deep breaths to slow your heart rate down a little, slow your breathing down a little, and get yourself a little more under control."

—*Butch Harmon, member of* Golf Digest*'s*
professional advisory staff

susan**anton**

Singer, performer, model, and avid golfer

Golf is most beautiful and offers its greatest lesson of life when you realize you are never, ever, ever out of the game. You are never out of the game unless you take yourself out of the game. It's just like life. I cannot tell you how many times I've had a really great round going and I get to the one hole that is my nemesis and I stand over the ball in a survival mode.

I realize even then, when I hit the ball in the canyon or in the water, that I'm not out of the hole. Just like life. If I lose my job, it doesn't mean I'm not going to find a better one the next day and that the loss wasn't a blessing. I can't tell you the number of times I've hit a hideous tee shot, dribbled it off the tee, and then I hit a fairway wood, chipped up, and saved par! Now I'm feeling great. Golf gets really interesting when you see how you can save the hole.

One of the greatest things I love in regard to golf or life in general is how you respond to the question: Do you choose the problem or do you choose the answer? The second you choose the answer, you don't have a problem. I read this in a series of books entitled *Course in Miracles*. When I read it, I thought, That is brilliant. We can choose the problem or we can choose the answer. They cannot coexist.

"Disaster in golf is really like life.
You just assess the situation and say,
'Okay. What do I do?' "

—*Susan Anton*

"You can't win a major on Thursday, Friday,
or Saturday, but you can certainly lose it
on those days."

—*Peter Jacobsen, back-to-back Johnnie Walker Cup champion*

"When disaster strikes, instead of using a
driver on the next hole, use your 3-wood. Make
your bogey or your par on the next hole
by playing it safe. Back off all your shots
until you get back into your rhythm."

—*Bill Roy, head pro at the Country Club of Green Valley, Arizona*

pat**goss**

Golf coach at Northwestern University

We try to set the precedent with our players that how you handle your bad golf defines you as a golfer. We all have days when we wake up on the right side of the bed and our girlfriend's treating us great and things are just wonderful. It's a beautiful day, we're playing a golf course that sets up well for us, we're excited to be there, and our golf clubs feel like silk in our hands. Anybody can go out on that day and play well.

However, the day you wake up on the wrong side of the bed, nothing's going right, your golf clubs feel like four-pound weights, and you're playing a golf course that isn't set up for your game, you immediately think your ability to score and compete on that particular day is going to define you.

You cannot accept bad golf. You have to decide you can control it. We try to instill in our players this pride in their bad golf. I think that's one of the first steps toward overcoming disaster. You learn you can handle those shaky three- or four-hole stretches. Keep it in play, go down a club, bunt it around, do anything to make sure you shoot a 72. You can do it.

"When disaster strikes, go back to your mindset, your comfort level."

—Tom Addis, former president of the PGA of America

"When you have to hit between two trees you seem to concentrate a little harder. Maybe that's what you should do when you're hitting a normal shot, concentrate a little harder."

—Luke Donald, 1999 NCAA Player of the Year from Northwestern University

jack**lemmon**

Still trying to make the cut in the AT&T at Pebble Beach

When I get in trouble is when I hit my best shots. I look at them and say, "You're going to make this one," and more than 50 percent of the time I do. It's the old theory: It's 50 percent air. Behind the tree, I don't care. I just hit it.

I probably concentrate more on difficult shots. The one thing I try to do is finish the shot and not get in a hurry and look up quick. That's the main thing. That's what most amateurs do when they've got a trouble shot. They hit it and halfway through the shot, their head's coming up already to take a look.

> **"I've always thought with a trouble shot, whether it's the Masters or the U.S. Open or the AT&T, it's best to be aggressive."**
>
> *—Peter Jacobsen, 1995 AT&T Pebble Beach champion*

andy**williams**

Singer and longtime host of a PGA tournament

Performing at a peak level is a combination of mind and talent. There are certainly guys with a lot of talent who don't seem to pull it together. I've often wondered why there couldn't be some way for all golfers to pull themselves together when they start falling apart. Perhaps it would be a hypnotist who would say, "When you get this feeling that you're losing it, count to twenty." Anything to get back into your normal way of playing.

A lot of times players fall apart in the last three or four holes if it's getting really close. It bothers me when the tournament leader is coming down the stretch and he loses his concentration or focus. Why does he lose it? What can he do to get back into that frame of mind he's always in? It has to be the mind.

It's the same in the world of entertainment. Everybody I know gets out of their focus when they're performing in a particular arena they're not used to. Maybe it's performing for the king or queen of England or doing a special night that's different from what they're used to doing. They'll fall apart! We all do it. There's a certain point when you lose your enthusiasm or your energy, and you don't perform very well. You don't care. If you get frightened you can't perform well.

I was playing with Lee Trevino at Indian Wells in the Bob

Hope Classic and I was on the driving range, which is right next to the first tee. I was practicing when I heard my name, "Andy Williams on the tee." I thought, Oh God, and I rushed over. I was so nervous, playing with Lee Trevino and not being clear about what I was going to do on the first tee. I put the ball down and Lee said, "Hurry. C'mon. Where have you been?"

I swung and hit my ball and he said, "Great shot. That was a wonderful shot." We got out there and Lee said, "I can't find your ball. I know where everybody's ball is but I can't find yours. The only thing here is a range ball."

There was a range ball with two red stripes around it that I had hit. I didn't even notice it when I put it on the tee because I was so nervous. Lee started shouting over to the second tee to Arnold Palmer. He said, "Hey, Arnie! Andy was so nervous he hit a range ball!" I was so embarrassed.

The first time I played in the Crosby, I was on the 18th hole and there were about two thousand people around the green. I looked up and the announcers were waving at me from the TV booth and Phil Harris was standing next to them. All the camera guys were the same ones who were doing my show at NBC and they were waving at me. I had this forty-five-foot putt. I was so nervous, I lost all my energy and just stood over the ball. Finally somebody said, "Andy, you've got to putt." I'd been over it for about a minute. I did a stroke and hit my toe and knocked the ball straight the opposite way. Everybody went, "Ooooooo." It sounded like a big upchuck, like "Auahhhh." It was pathetic. It was really pathetic. I reached the depths. I really did.

lee**trevino**

Member of six U.S. Ryder Cup teams

Trouble shots are all trial and error. If you're under a tree trying some godawful shot to get out of there, and you're going for the green and you've never, ever tried hitting such a shot, my suggestion is to take a wedge, hit it out sideways, and get back in play.

There's no reason to enter a marathon if you know you can only run one hundred yards. If you've never tried the shot before, don't try it now. Golfers have to try trouble shots to be able to execute them when they're playing golf. The only way to do that is practice. You don't have to hit many of them, just enough to say, "Hey, I've done this before."

The best advice I can give someone when he gets in trouble is to remember it's only one shot. Get the ball back in the fairway, put it on the green, make par or bogey. If you try to make a great shot, chances are bogey would be the best you'd make anyway. But if you try this crazy shot you're adding the possibility of a triple bogey.

"Some of us like to play Tarzan. We like to be creative and think we can do some things we really can't. That's the fun of the game."

—*Fuzzy Zoeller, who whistles while he works*

"You've got to have the guts not to be afraid to screw up. The guys who win are the ones who are not afraid to mess up. And that comes right from the heart."

—*Fuzzy Zoeller, winner of the 1979 Masters, the first year he qualified*

jean**vandevelde**

Runner-up at the 1999 British Open

People wonder how I have handled my British Open experience so well. What could I have done? Sat down somewhere and cried? What for? Life goes on. I look around and everybody has his share of problems. There are a lot of worse things happening. Besides, millions of people would have liked to have been in my position. Starting off Sunday's round I was three ahead. I didn't win it, but out of a hundred times that I'm three ahead, I'm going to win maybe ninety-five or ninety-seven times. I'll be happy with that. So, I have no right to complain.

Although the experience is in the past I'm not saying I never think about it, but I try to think about it in a positive way. If I only focused on the bad things that happen, such as on that last hole, I'd never be able to recuperate or even play golf again. So I concentrate more on what I did right on seventy-one holes, especially the last thirty-five, because I was leading the tournament for thirty-six holes. I try to learn from that. On the last hole someone up there said it wasn't my time. I think I was a bit unlucky as well, if you look at my second shot. But there's not much I can do about that.

johnny**miller**

1976 British Open champion

The biggest problem people have is they either try to look too heroic or they want to say, "At least I went for it." Like Jean Van de Velde in the British Open. If I were caddying for him, I would have told the ABC camera, "Look over here." I'd have broken the driver and broken the 3-wood, the 2-iron, the 3-iron, the 4-iron, the 5-iron, and then I'd say, "Jean, now you can play the hole with your 6-iron to the wedge." Hit the 6-iron, 8-iron, pitching wedge, three-putt, and win the tournament. But the thing is, players want to look like they're Sir Lancelot.

mark**loomis**

Scratch golfer, now a television sports producer

I was the replay producer for ABC Sports' coverage of the 1999 British Open at Carnoustie and I actually think Jean Van de Velde got a bad rap. What he did was not smart, but I think Van de Velde stood on the first tee that week and said, "I'm going to play this course as aggressively as I can possibly play it. I'm going to hit it as far as I can possibly hit it, because it's so narrow anyway. If I continue to hit good shots, even if I'm in the rough, I'll just be that much closer to the green."

He followed that thought all the way through and it worked for seventy-one holes. It didn't work on the 72nd hole. He tried it off the tee on the 18th hole on Sunday and it didn't work. I think at that point he should have said, "Wait a minute. I have a three-shot lead. I need to be smart. I got lucky with this tee shot, so let me just get back on the fairway and then I'll knock it on the green."

What people forget, though, is that when Paul Lawrie came to that same hole later that day in the playoff he could have laid up and still won. But he hit a 4-iron to ten feet, made birdie, and won by a couple of shots.

It's hard for me to say Jean Van de Velde was a big dummy. When I was watching, it was probably the most painful thing

I've ever seen on a golf course. You just wanted to grab the guy and say, "Stop! Don't do this!" But I think he had been in that aggressive mindset from the first hole on the first day, and he couldn't get out of it.

> **"Losing the British Open was not the end of the world. It is, after all, still just golf."**
>
> —*Jean Van de Velde*

> **"The secret is not hitting every shot perfect. The secret is getting the most out of the shots you don't hit perfect."**
>
> —*Ben Hogan, winner of all four major championships*

chapter nine

Heat
of Battle

"You feel like you want to
hit that perfect shot. You feel
the pressure but it's helping
you play better."

*—Nancy Lopez, recipient of
USGA's 1998 Bob Jones
Award*

lee**trevino**

*Winner of either a PGA or Senior PGA
tournament in five consecutive decades*

I actually concentrate much better when I get in the hunt. If you look at my record, anytime I had the lead going into the back nine I won 95 percent of the time. In fact, I can't ever remember any tournament where I had the lead with nine holes to play that I lost! Maybe I did somewhere down the line but I don't remember any.

In the hunt you tend to concentrate a lot better. You start weighing the percentages. If I try this shot, what's the percentage that I'll execute this shot? What's the percentage that I don't? Then you go with the highest percentage. Listen, we're not made out of steel. I've come down that pike on 15, 16, 17, and 18 with enough cotton in my mouth to knit a sweater. I couldn't whistle or spit. I've drunk seventeen gallons of water and it was all right in my belly; you could hear it when I took a swing, and it sounded like a fishing boat.

When I'm not contending, that's when I shoot my worst scores. When you've won as much as I have, the only thing that's important is winning. I don't give a damn about second or third or fourth or fifth. That doesn't mean a thing to me, so I tend to clown around a little bit and take more chances. I make a lot more mistakes when I'm not in contention.

peter**jacobsen**

Member of two U.S. Ryder Cup teams

The heat of battle is where you start to see a player's make-up. The great players go beyond fear. I think of Lee Trevino because I've played with him when he was on the hot seat and he was still talking and laughing and joking. Things could be melting all around him but he stood there and hit shot after shot after shot. Fuzzy Zoeller also comes to mind, as do people like Jack Nicklaus, Tiger Woods, Seve Ballesteros, Greg Norman, and Tom Watson, who all are a little bit cold-blooded.

People say, "Oh, you can't be jovial and win." Well, I can point out a lot of great players like Trevino and Fuzzy, who won a lot of major championships, and they were laughing the whole way around. But I can also point out players who didn't crack a smile and just rode that icy glare.

I won't say it's a mean stare or a mean streak, but it's all business, right to the title. It all depends on your personality, but I definitely believe that the guys who win are the guys who say, "Hey, look. I'm going to win this. I don't care what people say. It's a 4-iron. I can hit this right at the flag. I've done it before. I can do it and I'm going to do it right now." They may be joking when they say it or they may be really serious inside, but either way, they challenge themselves. When you challenge yourself, it's more personal.

"I just try to hit the damn thing."

—Jack Lemmon, Peter's partner at the AT&T

greg**norman**

First PGA Tour player to surpass $10 million in winnings

I strive to be in the heat of the battle. That's what I cherish the most. There's no better feeling than having your mind in total control of your body, in control of everything that's going on. It's so hard to describe. I wish people could feel it.

I know what it's like when Tiger Woods or Jack Nicklaus goes down the fairway, or somebody who is playing great golf is winning, because I've been there.

It's such an incredibly difficult feeling to express because your mind is so much at peace when you're in control of your game. It's so peaceful, so relaxing. Things just go at a slow pace. It seems like four hours of golf takes only forty minutes.

"It's still fun."

—*Greg Norman*

"When you're really on, a calmness comes over you."

—*Mark O'Meara,* Golf Digest *playing editor*

mark**o'meara**

1998 Masters and British Open champion

I remember the back nine at the '98 Masters. I kept telling myself, "Look, this is not a life-or-death situation. My life's going to go on, no matter what happens."

I've always looked at coming down the stretch as a battle, where every shot becomes important. You're fighting a miniwar between not only your technique and your mental attitude, but also between the golf course and your competitors. You have no control over what your competition is doing. You only have control over you, so you're trying not to make any major mistakes or get in your own way.

At the Masters I tried to use some of my past experience and to remind myself that I had won before and I should be able to do it again. It's funny because many times I had watched players on the 18th green at Augusta hole an eight-foot putt, and I wondered, "How could anybody conjure up enough nerve to hole a putt on the last hole at the Masters? It's just amazing." For some reason, I holed one of the biggest putts of my life on the 18th and one that's going to be very memorable in Masters history.

hale**irwin**

Winner of three U.S. Opens, 1974, 1979, and 1990

The first word that comes to mind when you're in the heat of battle is urgency. A sense of urgency coupled with a good healthy dose of confidence. You have to have the confidence in yourself to know you're capable of winning, but you need to draw a line between being confident and being a braggadocio. At least for me, cockiness doesn't work. Confidence does. I don't want to go beyond that because then you start assuming things that are not assumable. You might make a false judgment that your opponent will fail, and that you will succeed. Those assumptions are all judgmental and I don't think you can judge and still give your opponent respect. If you don't have respect for your opponent, I find it hard to believe you will have respect for yourself.

Certainly I get nervous. The funny things wandering in my head are good things. I enjoy that level of anxiety. I don't think I could be satisfied playing for twentieth or thirtieth. If I'm not going to be in the arena where I feel like I can be good enough, then it's time to think of doing something else.

During the heat of battle I don't think I necessarily change that much. The experience factor sets in. Your training kicks in to tell you you can't be someone who you're not. If you're the quiet type, you can't suddenly be talking. If you're the talkative type, you can't suddenly be quiet. I don't think it's a winning formula to go outside the personality that you are on the other sixty-eight or sixty-nine holes and suddenly become someone else on the last few.

When I'm playing within myself and doing the right things and concentrating on the task at hand, I don't hear any more or any less. Thinigs I want to hear I may hear more acutely. Things I want to see I may see more clearly. Because for the most part, if you're listening and hearing all the peripheral sounds, you're looking for a reason not to succeed. You're not focused on the task at hand.

When I win it's more of a celebration than a relief. If you're struggling and you're backing into a win, you may feel relief, but if you're playing the way you're capable of and you're doing the things you're confident you can do, then you want that to continue. That high lasts forever. There's no way of taking it away, but the adrenaline surge is gone probably within twenty-four hours.

steve**elkington**

Twice Australian Amateur champion, 1980 and 1981

Once you've won a few times, instead of all the anxiety that comes to you on about 14, about whether you're going to be able to finish it off, you realize someone's going to win the tournament. You tell yourself, "Stay in the game. Don't throw your cards in yet."

I learned from Jackie Burke, who said, "You're trying to win the tournament. Just get in the playoff. If there are two guys tied with you at the end, and you get in a playoff, one guy may faint and the other guy may hit it in the woods. You never know."

You have to be careful. Don't think you have to win the tournament on every hole. A lot of guys who have finally broken through have said, "You know what? I actually did less coming in than I thought I would ever have to."

> **"The only guy I'm playing in the last two rounds of the U.S. Open is myself."**
>
> *—Tom Watson, 1982 U.S. Open champion*

gary**m^ccord**

Twice PGA Senior Tour's Player of the Month

When you're in contention on the back nine during the final round, don't beat yourself; try to let the other guys beat themselves. There are not many heroic shots involved. You don't come to the last hole and hit a 1-iron to two feet and win. You just get out there, and somehow everybody else is falling by the wayside and you come out on top.

That's how I've won my senior tournaments, by just hanging around, getting the ball in the fairway, getting the ball on the green. Give yourself a chance to make the putt. Don't do anything dumb. Don't miss the shot on the wrong side. Just don't let any of that bad stuff get in your way.

"You know what's amazing? You don't hear anything. Everything's kind of muffled. When you're really concentrating, a bomb could go off and you wouldn't hear it. It's incredible how the mind affects your game. It truly is."

—*Fuzzy Zoeller, 1984 U.S. Open champion*

annika**sorenstam**

World Amateur champion in 1992

The most exciting thing in a tournament is to be in the hunt. I always look forward to Sunday afternoon as a chance to win. The adrenaline is pumping and it's just something that happens naturally. Your heart is pumping so fast. You may have sweaty hands and you're talking really fast, but it's a matter of controlling it when you need to.

Many times I've come down the stretch and the adrenaline is so strong, I have to hit a club less. I walk fast and my caddie will say, "Slow down. Take your time, be patient. You'll get to hit the shot." It's a matter of controlling the shot you want to hit at the particular time. It's very easy to get anxious.

It's a lot of fun to be in this situation. I love it. Sometimes I'm able to pull through and sometimes I'm not. Even though I've done it several times, every time is a new experience. It's always different. You're swinging a different way and the course is different. You get into your own little world. You are so into you. You are so into your next shot. I don't really pay any attention to my opponent. It's just a matter of doing my work. Get the ball in the hole. That's it.

roger**maltbie**

During rookie year on PGA Tour in 1975,
won back-to-back titles

'll always remember the back nine on Sunday at the first Memorial tournament, Jack Nicklaus's tournament. Gosh, I was playing a game. Back then I just loved competition. It was nerve-wracking, but there are those who shy away from that and there are those who love it. Obviously Tiger loves it. I don't know if I love it like Tiger does, because I don't think I have the skills Tiger has. It's hard to love it when you don't know which barrel the ball's going to come out of. But I loved what happened in the Memorial.

I was ahead after fifty-four holes at four under par, and I shot 76 in the last round. The golf course is brutally hard. At even par I tied with Hale Irwin and we were in a playoff. Jack had wanted a three-hole playoff. It was the first and only three-hole playoff on the Tour. He felt his event should not be decided by sudden death. Television eventually didn't go for it, so there was never another one.

We went to the 15th hole, which was a par-5, in order to play 15, 16, and 17. If we were still even, we would go to 18, which is what we eventually did. I won it on the fourth extra hole. As we went out to the 15th, here was Hale Irwin, a U.S. Open champion, a great player, and here I was, a long-haired, mustached kid from California. It was pretty obvious from little remarks Jack had made and what was written in the papers that Jack wanted Hale to win his event. It would be a great validation of his tournament if a great player won, and by no means was I a great player.

We stood at the 15th tee and I said, "Good luck to you, Hale," and he kind of smirked in that Hale Irwin way, and my caddie, Jeff Burrell, hit me with his elbow and said, "This guy thinks he's going to win!" I started to laugh. I laughed hysterically because Jeff knew Hale was better than me, I knew Hale was better than me, all the fans knew Hale was better. There wasn't any secret who was the underdog. Suddenly it just became a game, and I was fine.

We both birdied the first hole, followed with par, par, and then I birdied again at 18 to win. I can't play the game any other way. I can only speak for myself, but golf has to be fun. Look at Trevino. When he's laughing and joking, he's playing great. When he's tight-lipped, he's not. As long as I'm playing a game and having fun, I usually play better.

Bob Rotella once gave me a great quote. He said, "You have to remember: Trying your hardest is not necessarily trying your best." It's really true. It's the American way. If things don't go your way, you try harder. You work harder. You hit twice as many balls. What happens is you get so tight, you can't do anything.

wally**goodwin**

Former Stanford University golf coach

Notah Begay always wanted to do things differently. He was the most fun kid to have around because if there was a different way to do anything, he'd figure it out—whatever it was, in golf or anything else. He has an extraordinary imagination in terms of golf shots and he's a great athlete—a great basketball player, a great soccer player, and a wonderful golfer. So he has all that going for him.

Notah was flamboyant. He'd think, I'll show these guys how well I'm playing by how many different kinds of shots I can hit today. I'll never forget the year we won the National Championship in Texas and Notah was coming to the 18th hole, where the preceding three kids from Texas (with whom we were duking it out that day) had knocked their balls in the water.

All I was trying to do was to get my players to hit over to the left. Play on dry land. So I'm pleading with Notah, "Hey, Notah, don't do anything fantastic. Just hit a nice little cut shot down the left side. Play it safe because it looks like we've got this tournament won." He winks at me, takes out his driver, whips it over the water, right to left, lands it right in the middle of the fairway, puts his driver in his bag, and waves to me. That was Notah, and that was a very lovable aspect of the kid.

Notah could hit the ball a variety of different ways. He probably didn't have all the shots Tiger has but he had at least as good a wedge game from seemingly impossible places as anybody I've ever seen play. In the National Championship, the year we were trying to repeat, he had a couple of short game shots to save par that were so unbelievable, you had to sort of pinch yourself to make sure you were awake and actually saw the shot.

He loved to show everybody what he could do. One time at Hilton Head, he was playing with NCAA champion Todd Demsey and some other guy. They were playing a long par-5 with a big dogleg to the right, and his second shot was over the swamps and onto a green that doesn't run away from you. It's just a big, wide, shallow green, with a big trap in front. He took out his 2-iron, which had always been enough club to make the green. He whipped it up there but it went in low and bounced into the trap.

I was on the left side of the fairway, walking, watching this performance. He dropped his bag, took his 2-iron, looked over to make sure Todd Demsey was watching, nodded at him, walked into the trap with his two-iron, laid it back like a wedge, and hit it up, about four feet from the hole. Well, you know that's disconcerting. But he was that kind of a guy, wonderful to be with, a great friend, all the way through.

ken**blanchard**

Author of The One Minute Golfer
and founder of the Golf University

Have you read that wonderful book *The Last Journey*, about a journalist whose father was dying of cancer? He took his father to Scotland for one last golf trip. Ever since he had grown up, he and his dad had been really competitive against each other. They had a wonderful time playing but now his dad was dying of cancer. He said, "Dad, I want you to organize what kind of game we want to play." His dad said, "Son, while we're over here, why don't we play NATO golf?" The son asked, "What do you mean by 'NATO golf'?" His dad answered, "Not Attached To Outcome."

There's a really interesting thing about NATO golf. If you look at the future, present, past scenario, you should be playing one shot at a time and not beating your head, worrying about the outcome. Get into the dance and the process of making the shot, don't worry about the outcome. Go for where you're going. Let it fly without saying, "Don't hook it, stupid," or "There are trees over there." You play much better when you're not concerned about the outcome of each shot. Merely have an interest in what's going to happen on this one. How do I let this beauty fly? *Not Attached To Outcome*. It's quite a concept.

gene**littler**

Three-time consecutive winner of the
Tournament of Champions

I never thought I was going to win a tournament, until I got into one and I was playing well. I never felt before it began, Geez, I'm playing so well, I'm going to win this thing. Never. I would just gut it out and do the best I could.

The first year I won the Tournament of Champions, a sportswriter called me on Saturday night; I had a ten-shot lead. That was one I thought I could win. He said, "I'm writing an article and I'd like to ask you, what's the biggest lead you ever blew?" I said, "I really don't want to talk about that. Thank you very much." Click, I hung up. I mean, what a question! I don't remember who he was but I still remember his question forty-five years later. I didn't need to think about that.

In the heat of battle you feed on what you've done in the past. It depends on how you're playing at the time. You still have to rely on something and in my case it was, "Keep the tempo good." If I did that, I thought I had a pretty good shot because I wasn't going to go too fast. That falls into the category of mental thinking. You have to be thinking about something.

"You train yourself for the heat of battle. You always wonder how you're going to perform when you get into that position, and you don't know until you actually get there. You have to be in control of yourself at all times and if you're not in control of yourself, you're not going to be there at the end."

—Billy Casper, 1983 U.S. Senior Open champion

"In the heat of the battle, you need somebody to remind you to remain on an even keel with your same routine. Do things that are repetitive."

—Dale Walker, golf coach at San Diego State University

curtis**strange**

Winner of seventeen PGA tour events and ABC golf analyst

When I was trying to win my second U.S. Open in a row, I came off the 18th tee with a one-shot lead and I found myself speaking out loud to keep my mind from wavering. I didn't want to think about the trophy or about what the U.S. Open means, or of all the people who helped me along the way. I said to my caddie, "Okay, Greg, three more shots, three more shots. Just three more shots." We said that aloud, all the way down the fairway. He did his part and I did mine, just to outwardly reinforce what we were thinking. It worked that time. I don't know if it worked for that reason, but it kept me from thinking about two in a row and what it would mean to me.

The number one priority at that time was to do everything I could to win. I always felt like I went at it maybe a little harder than some. You can't get inside anybody else's mind, so you only know what you did. When you're in contention all of your senses are at their utmost. That's why you see some of the most incredible athletic endeavors. That's why you see some players hit poor shots because they can't handle it and other players hit the most spectacular golf shots.

You believe you can do something very few other people can do. Arrogance comes into it; certainly it's self-centered. To be the best in the world, all of those things have to be involved. To come down to the last hole of the U.S. Open and birdie and win in front of the world is something special. To see an athlete perform at that level, under those circumstances is truly extraordinary.

Why a player performs under pressure at the last hole and why he doesn't is fascinating. You see the same players hitting outstanding shots under pressure and you see the same guys playing great Thursday, Friday, part of Saturday, and then folding. It's interesting to me because they're intelligent and nice people. That's part of it, too. You have to have a little bit of a mean streak and you have to have an arrogance to put your ass on the line. You've got to have an arrogance to think you're good enough to make the last shot.

You also need the guts to realize you can't do it all the time and you're going to miss some. When you miss, you say, "That's okay, I'll get it the next time." I always loved that. I always felt, "Give me the ball. I want the last shot." That was me personally. I wanted the last shot. I knew I wasn't going to make them all, but I was going to make some. That's the fun of athletics, of golf.

Winning in itself is tough, and when you're struggling and not playing your best and you've done everything in your power to get the ball in the hole or to beat the next guy, it's exhausting. You have to try so much harder and concentrate so much more and not let any negatives creep in. You have to tell yourself constantly, "I can do this. I can do this. I'm better than this guy. I'm the best. I'm going to hit this shot in front of all these people. I want center stage at the last hole. I want that chance." You have to believe it and you have to like it, too. A lot of the guys who have great talent don't like that.

Players will pay the price but then they get there and they don't like it. Maybe they're not arrogant enough. Maybe they're not secure enough. To be on that stage on the last green at any tournament, much less a major, is fun.

I always thought you practice your whole life to get there, so don't back off at the last second. But people do. Some are afraid of winning. It can be interpreted a lot of different ways. It's a broad-based phrase but it's pretty accurate: They're afraid of being on center stage on the last hole. They're insecure about their abilities, insecure about themselves, insecure about what this might bring to them. They have a nice career now and per-haps they don't want to be "the next guy."

"Everybody plays golf to his personality."

—Simon Bevan, head pro at Glen Abbey Golf Club,
Oakland, Ontario

butch**harmon**

*Head pro at Crow Valley Golf Club, Iowa,
in the late 1970s*

The heat of the battle is where you'll find the biggest differ-ence between the really good golfers and the also-rans. The really good ones love it. They thrive on it. That's what they live for. The Tiger Woodses, the Jack Nicklauses, the Tom Watsons, the Lee Trevinos, the Curtis Stranges. They live for this situation. They want to come down to the last hole and have to hit the shot to win the tournament.

There are other players who would never, ever want to have that shot. We've had a lot of great players on the Tour who win the majority of their tournaments by shooting 65 on Sunday, coming from four or five back because they feel very relaxed. However, you give them the lead and they don't feel relaxed.

Tiger Woods is the exception to that rule. He loves to lead. In his mind, he says, "I know I'm better than you are and you're not going to come get me." There are other people who get the lead and can't handle it. They start thinking negatively. They start playing too conservatively.

The key is you have to stick to what got you there. You can't try to do anything different. Stick to the things you know.

Understand your own capabilities. Know what you can do and what you can't do and don't try to do things you can't do on the golf course. That's the simplest way to put it.

> **"You just have to believe in yourself and have the attitude that you can do it. You have to stand on the first tee and think you can win."**
>
> *—Lori Kane, Canadian golfer and winner of the LPGA's*
> *2000 Michelob Light Classic*

> **"Sometimes we get so afraid of hitting bad shots, we don't let ourselves hit good ones."**
>
> *—Butch Harmon, Tiger Woods's coach*

ken**venturi**

1964 U.S. Open champion and television golf commentator

Ben Hogan always said, "I've hit this shot a thousand times, and the shot is still the same, no matter if you're playing for fun, a club championship, a Tour tournament, or for the U.S. Open."

Hogan spoke of Karl Wallenda, "The Great Wallenda," perhaps the greatest high-wire walker in the world, who walked the wire between New York City skyscrapers. When Wallenda was asked, "Do you get more nervous the higher they put the wire?" His answer was, "Why should I? The wire never changes."

That puts the whole thing in perspective. Hogan said, "I've hit it a thousand times. Why should I be nervous? The wire never changes." That is one of the great pronouncements of all time. It is so profound. It truly sums it up. When you get to the 18th hole, do you get more nervous because it's the last hole? Why should you? *The wire never changes.* I think that's the best golf statement I've ever heard.

"To win, you must play your best golf
when you need it and your sloppy stuff
when you can afford it. I shall not explain
how you achieve this timing."

—*Bobby Jones, first player to win four majors in the same year*

"I remember my grandfather once pulled
me aside when I was a young man and said,
'It doesn't look like you're going to be that
good a golfer, so make sure you play fast.' "

—*George Bush, former president of the United States*

"There is money you earn as salary,
bonuses, investments, interest, theft;
and then there's money that you win
playing golf. Now that's real money."

—*Bill Murray, star of* Caddyshack

Index